TRADE IN CLASSICAL A

Historians have long argued about the place of trade in classical antiquity: was it the life-blood of a complex, Mediterranean-wide economic system, or a thin veneer on the surface of an underdeveloped agrarian society? Trade underpinned the growth of Athenian and Roman power, helping to supply armies and cities. It furnished the goods that ancient elites needed to maintain their dominance – and yet, those same elites generally regarded trade and traders as a threat to social order. Trade, like the patterns of consumption that determined its development, was implicated in wider debates about politics, morality and the state of society, just as the expansion of trade in the modern world is presented both as the answer to global poverty and as an instrument of exploitation and cultural imperialism. This book explores the nature and importance of ancient trade, considering its ecological and cultural significance as well as its economic aspects.

NEVILLE MORLEY is Reader in Ancient Economic History and Historical Theory at the University of Bristol. His previous publications include *Metropolis and Hinterland: the City of Rome and the Italian Economy* (Cambridge University Press, 1996) and *Models and Concepts in Ancient History* (2004).

KEY THEMES IN ANCIENT HISTORY

EDITORS

P. A. Cartledge
Clare College, Cambridge
P. D. A. Garnsey
Jesus College, Cambridge

Key Themes in Ancient History aims to provide readable, informed and original studies of various basic topics, designed in the first instance for students and teachers of Classics and Ancient History, but also for those engaged in related disciplines. Each volume is devoted to a general theme in Greek, Roman, or where appropriate, Graeco-Roman history, or to some salient aspect or aspects of it. Besides indicating the state of current research in the relevant area, authors seek to show how the theme is significant for our own as well as ancient culture and society. By providing books for courses that are oriented around themes it is hoped to encourage and stimulate promising new developments in teaching and research in ancient history.

Other books in the series

Death-ritual and social structure in classical antiquity, by Ian Morris
0 521 37465 0 (hardback), 0 521 37611 4 (paperback)

Literacy and orality in ancient Greece, by Rosalind Thomas
0 521 37346 8 (hardback), 0 521 37742 0 (paperback)

Slavery and society at Rome, by Keith Bradley
0 521 37287 9 (hardback), 0 521 36887 7 (paperback)

Law, violence, and community in classical Athens, by David Cohen
0 521 38167 3 (hardback), 0 521 38837 6 (paperback)

Public order in ancient Rome, by Wilfried Nippel
0 521 38327 7 (hardback), 0 521 38748 3 (paperback)

Friendship in the classical world, by David Konstan
0 521 45402 6 (hardback), 0 521 45998 2 (paperback)

Sport and society in ancient Greece, by Mark Golden
0 521 49698 5 (hardback), 0 521 49790 6 (paperback)

Food and society in classical antiquity, by Peter Garnsey
0 521 64182 9 (hardback), 0 521 64588 3 (paperback)

TRADE IN CLASSICAL ANTIQUITY

NEVILLE MORLEY

CAMBRIDGE
UNIVERSITY PRESS

CAMBRIDGE UNIVERSITY PRESS
Cambridge, New York, Melbourne, Madrid, Cape Town, Singapore, São Paulo, Delhi

Cambridge University Press
The Edinburgh Building, Cambridge CB2 8RU, UK

Published in the United States of America by Cambridge University Press, New York

www.cambridge.org
Information on this title: www.cambridge.org/9780521634168

First published 2007

A catalogue record for this publication is available from the British Library

ISBN 978-0-521-63279-9 hardback
ISBN 978-0-521-63416-8 paperback

Transferred to digital printing 2009

For Anne

Contents

Preface

As I was completing this book, in the weeks after Hurricane Katrina struck New Orleans, the price of petrol in some parts of the United Kingdom reached £1 per litre; this was, in part, because the destruction of refining facilities in the Gulf of Mexico meant that American oil companies were seeking to buy up supplies in Europe, while the price of crude oil on the global market passed $70 per barrel. This can be seen as an indication of the awesome power of the modern world-trade system to mobilise goods from across the globe; there is a shortfall in supply leading to a price rise, the news is communicated almost instantaneously and the market responds, shipping oil thousands of miles to where the demand is greatest. The demands of resentful road hauliers that the government should intervene to lower prices and protect their profits are based on a complete misunderstanding of basic economics; the market simply reflects the hard realities of supply and demand, and petrol subsidies or a reduction in fuel tax could defeat their own object by stimulating demand and pushing prices up even further. Such developments emphasise the relative powerlessness of states, let alone individuals, in the face of market forces; they are a forcible reminder that, within a globalised economy, even the basic rhythms of everyday life can now be affected by events thousands of miles away – an experience which, as a regular buyer of *Fairtrade* products, I naively tend to associate more with downtrodden coffee and cocoa producers in the Third World. Connectivity, it is clear, affects us all; however much the rules of the game are rigged in favour of certain players, no one is wholly insulated from the effects of the global market.

Over the last decade, as I have been working on this book, the terms in which trade, markets and 'globalisation' are discussed have been changing. There remain many adherents of the conventional view of trade as indispensable and unequivocally desirable, the lifeblood of economic development and the sole hope for lifting millions out of poverty; the market, it is argued, is the only efficient way of allocating and distributing limited resources. Some governments, above all those of the United States and the United Kingdom, continue to follow the advice of such economists, working to free world trade from its remaining constraints and to extend the reach of market forces further into social life. Increasingly, however, more critical voices have made themselves heard, not least in protests at meetings of the World Trade Organisation and G8 summits. Far from being a cure for poverty, trade is seen to be widening the gap between rich and poor. The globalised market creates misery for agricultural producers in Africa and South America, sweatshop workers in Asia and unemployed steel workers in South Wales; consumer demand for strawberries in December, perfectly round red tomatoes (however tasteless) and dirt-cheap meat (however toxic) destroys eco-systems and racks up the food miles; the relentless pursuit of profit undermines local social and economic structures, while even culture and knowledge become commodities. These developments are attributed not to trade *per se* but to the conditions under which it currently takes place – depending on the commentator, the blame lies with systems of agricultural tariffs, the dynamics of capitalism or dependence on carbon-based energy – but there is a general sense that more trade is not necessarily the answer to everything.

In particular, there is a feeling that the conventional understanding of trade, as simply a mechanism by which supply and demand are reconciled and resources are allocated in the most efficient way possible, neglects all the important questions about sustainability, justice, and the degree to which the market – as a reflection of the human beings whose decisions ultimately determine its operations – is not so much efficient as irrational and unpredictable. Recent events seem to confirm the need for cultural and psychological explanations alongside economic ones: petrol shortages created by panic-buying as the sight of other people queuing to buy petrol arouses a fear of shortages, and, underlying the whole problem, the way that individual car ownership has come to be seen as an inalienable and indispensable right, regardless of its social or environmental consequences. In such circumstances, the ancient idealisation of self-sufficiency and the avoidance of dependence, regularly blamed for the lack of economic development in classical antiquity, appears in a new light – but only to emphasise the impossibility of realising *autarkeia* in the modern world without a radical change of lifestyle. This is true even for those who attempt to recreate *The Good Life* in their back gardens. My chickens eat grain from the other side of the country, my beehives include components from Germany and China, and my home brew uses Czech hops and electricity from non-renewable sources; this book would not have been produced without Indian tea, German beer and sausages, a Japanese laptop built in the Philippines running an American operating system, and the ideas of scholars from across the globe. Ancient self-sufficiency, too, was more about asserting one's adherence to a set of values and adopting a social identity than a practical policy, but the gap between ideal and reality was not so great as it is today. It is a reminder that the sort of trade now permeating and shaping our lives is not a natural and universal institution, based on innate human tendencies, but a particular and, in the light of current events, probably limited cultural expression.

To most ancient historians, this contrast between past and present will appear a very unremarkable conclusion; in the great debate between 'primitivist' and 'modernising' approaches to the ancient economy, one side has constantly emphasised the enormous differences between ancient and modern societies. Underpinning this primitivist perspective, however, is a blanket acceptance of the conventional association of trade with economic development, an assumption it shares with the modernisers; for all their differences, both sides take it for granted that trade is an index of modernity (without properly exploring the meanings of that problematic concept), and that the proper questions to ask in a book like this are about the volume of trade, the nature of the objects traded and the degree to which the organisation of trade resembled that of medieval or early modern Europe. The problem is that either these questions are unanswerable, given the state and nature of the surviving evidence, or the answers offered fail to give any sense of what was distinctive about Greek or Roman antiquity as opposed to other pre-industrial societies, labelling them simply as 'non-modern' or 'proto-modern'.

This book seeks to set up and explore different questions, and to offer different perspectives on the subject of trade in classical antiquity and the nature of ancient economic structures. It draws on ideas that have been developed in economic history, environmental history, anthropology and sociology, and on the recent work of some ancient economic historians whose avowed intention is to get beyond the stale and unprofitable oppositions of the old debates. The result is a picture of antiquity that may appear relatively 'modern', in so far as it is difficult to imagine the development of classical culture without a high level of movement of goods through the Mediterranean – but only on condition that the present day is seen to be less modern, its economy less detached from the rest of society, than is generally claimed. In particular, the image of both ancient and modern is tinted by the fact that, as is becoming increasingly clear, connectivity has its costs as well as its undeniable benefits, and that some of those 'benefits' depend very much on one's place in the social structure.

This book has been a long time in the making, and I am fortunate that academic publishing – or at any rate the Classics section of Cambridge University Press – operates according to a system of relaxed, personalised exchange rather than insisting on the strict enforcement of written contracts and their notional deadlines. In such systems of reciprocity and trust, an obligation may finally be discharged years after it was initially incurred, when the debtor is finally in a position to repay what is owed and/or when the sense of shame and embarrassment at his failure to do so becomes overwhelming. It is with a feeling of enormous relief that I am finally able to thank Peter Garnsey, Paul Cartledge and Michael Sharp for their faith that I would, eventually, get round to finishing this book; I suspect they may often have wished that they had asked someone less susceptible to illness, family crisis and ever-expanding academic administrative duties.

I have incurred many further debts in the course of writing; for ideas, encouragement, loans of books and unpublished papers, conversations and prompt responses to random queries. I am particularly beholden to Sitta von Reden, for the example of her work, for the pleasure – now, unfortunately, in the past – of having her as a colleague, and for her sympathy as a fellow *Key Themes* defaulter. I have benefited enormously from seeing the draft chapters of fellow contributors to the forthcoming *Cambridge Economic History of Greco-Roman Antiquity*, especially those of Wim Jongman, Astrid Möller, Robin Osborne and Gary Reger, from the comments of the editors, especially Walter Scheidel, on my own chapter, and from participating in the related seminar. Seminar audiences in Bristol, Exeter and The Hague have made many helpful comments on early drafts of some of this material. The Bristol final-year students who survived my unit on 'Trade in Antiquity' in 2003/4 made clear to me the limitations both of existing approaches to the subject and of my attempts at developing a new agenda, and I owe them a great deal for that. Among many other friends and colleagues who have in one way or another contributed to this enterprise, I would like to single out Peter Bang, Gillian Clark, Shelley Hales, Aideen Hartney, Aleka Lianeri, Dominic Rathbone and Greg Woolf.

I am indebted to Jill Glover and Anna Hales, for personal support and sympathy at various stages over the last few years; to Elfi Dorsch and Hans Schmid for Bier, Kuchen und Mitgefühl in the latter stages of writing; to my favourite exotic luxury items, Amber, Basil, Cleo and Jasper; and above all and always to Anne, for everything.

CHAPTER I

Trade and the ancient economy

In the early second century BCE a ship arrived at the urban harbour of Pisa, having made its way up from North Africa via Sicily and Campania. Before it could be fully unloaded, however, it collided with part of the harbour structure, probably during a storm, and sank rapidly; at least one member of the crew went down with the vessel, along with some of the animals that made up an important part of its cargo. Over the years, tides dispersed most of the remains; the entire harbour became silted up and then forgotten until 1998, when preliminary construction work on a new regional headquarters for the Italian State Railway brought the complex back to light. Along with other harbour structures, and at least another fifteen vessels ranging in date from the third century BCE to the fifth century CE, archaeologists uncovered the damaged pier and some of the large timbers of the ship that had crashed into it, along with fragments of its cargo and the personal effects of its crew, and some human bones (Bruni 2000).

As in most ancient shipwrecks, the bulk of the finds were pottery. The ship had been carrying Graeco-Italic wine amphorae from the Campanian region, which provide the main evidence for its date, and Punic amphorae from North Africa that may, to judge from the number of pigs' shoulder bones found in the wreckage, have contained preserved pork joints. Other pottery found on board included four *thymiateria*, moulded terracotta incense burners, reinforcing the North African connection, along with black-glazed crockery from Volterra and two painted vases from Iberia. The contents of the amphorae may have been part of the crew's provisions rather than destined for trade; the ship's main cargo seems to have been livestock, since the archaeologists uncovered numerous bones in the wreckage, including those of three horses and a young lioness.

What does a shipwreck like this tell us about trade in classical antiquity? The answers that would be given by different historians vary widely – including the possibility that the ship had little to do with 'trade' as it is generally understood. It depends on the questions that we ask of such evidence, and, more importantly, on our assumptions about the nature of the ancient economy, which provide the context in which we interpret such a find. At the most basic level, we can simply note that particular objects were being moved from one area of the Mediterranean to another; and many historical accounts from the nineteenth and early twentieth centuries that deal with trade do focus on compiling lists of 'the objects of trade' as an end in itself. Such accounts relied more or less exclusively on literary evidence; when Pliny the Elder noted that, for example, Spanish wool was renowned for its pure black colour, it indicates that at the very least the wool was known outside its region of origin and probably was shipped into Rome (*Natural History* 8.190–3). H. J. Loane's *Industry and Commerce of the City of Rome* (1938) used such evidence to compile long lists of imports; drawing on Pliny (*NH* 8.53) and on historical accounts (including *SHA Hadr.* 19.5), she concluded that 'an import of considerable bulk that came with regularity to the urban docks were animals for the games at Rome' (1938: 55). Lions are said to come mainly from North Africa, with some from Syria; the first recorded import was in 186 BCE. The shipment of such animals was important enough to appear in iconography; a sarcophagus of the third century CE depicts a ship coming into port with three cages on deck, each containing a lion (Toynbee 1973: 61). Through the Pisa excavation, archaeology confirms and illustrates the literary record, with the import of a lioness in a ship that certainly came from North Africa and was probably Punic in origin, dating to not long after the trade is said to have begun.

THE GREAT DEBATE

The limitations of this approach to the subject are obvious; it is what M. I. Finley referred to as 'reportage and crude taxonomy, antiquarianism in its narrowest sense' (1985: 66). The literary evidence for the movement of goods is almost entirely confined to a few great cities such as Rome, Alexandria and Athens (in this context, the Pisa wreck offers a useful indication that the practice of holding wild-beast shows spread to other cities quite soon after their institution in the capital). Further, such an approach tells us little or nothing about the significance of such traffic; it cannot give any indication of its frequency (the sources note the exceptional, whether an exceptionally exotic import or some exceptionally lavish games, not the everyday), nor of its profitability or contribution to the urban economy relative to other goods, nor of its development over time (since it is necessary to draw together every fragment of evidence from every period). Historians of more recent periods can draw on detailed records of imports and exports on a year-by-year basis, charting the fortunes of a city's economy and even those of individual merchant families; ancient historians are left with the bald statement that Rome sometimes imported lions from Africa. Finley again: 'every statement or calculation to be found in an ancient text, every artefact finds a place, creating a morass of unintelligible, meaningless, unrelated "facts"' (1985: 61).

Such lists of imports have, however, acquired greater significance when incorporated into wider discussions of the development of the ancient economy as a whole. Taking a broader geographical and chronological perspective raises different questions: not whether we can chart the frequency and economic significance of the movement of a particular good to a particular location, but whether we can chart the development of 'trade and commerce' through the increasing frequency and diversity of traffic of all kinds. Shipments of lions to Italy are not important in themselves but rather as an indicator of the scale of movement of more basic goods – the tip of the iceberg, so to speak, which the sources record because of its exceptional nature while ignoring the vast amount of less glamorous activity taking place across the Mediterranean. A society which regularly transports lions from Africa to Italy must be one in which trade has developed to an impressive degree, across the empire. This is the picture of ancient commercial activity offered, for example, in M. I. Rostovtzeff's *Social and Economic History of the Roman Empire*:

In the second century, the commerce of Gaul and with it agriculture and industry reached an unprecedented state of prosperity. To realize the brilliant development of commerce and industry in Gaul, it is sufficient to read the inscriptions in the twelfth and thirteenth volumes of the *Corpus* [*Corpus Inscriptionum Latinarum*] and to study the admirable collection of sculptures and bas-reliefs found in the country . . . The inscriptions of Lyons, for example, whether engraved on stone monuments or on various items of common use ('*instrumenta domestica*'), and particularly those which mention the different trade associations, reveal the great importance of the part played by the city in the economic life of Gaul and of the Roman Empire as a whole. Lyons was not only the great clearing house for the commerce in corn, wine, oil, and lumber; she was also one of the largest centres in the Empire for the manufacture and distribution of most of the articles consumed by Gaul, Germany and Britain. (Rostovtzeff 1957: 165–6)

One might reasonably label such an approach to the ancient evidence as 'optimistic'. It is more commonly characterised as 'modernising', in so far as historians like Rostovtzeff not only identify a high level of economic activity in the Hellenistic and Roman periods but unselfconsciously regard it as basically comparable to more recent economic activity – 'the modern development, in this sense, differs from the ancient only in quantity and not in quality' (Rostovtzeff 1926: 10; cf. Hopkins 1983a; Cartledge 1998; Morley 2004: 33–50). 'Trade' as an activity is largely taken for granted as the expression of a natural human instinct to exchange goods and pursue profit; the movement of goods is automatically assumed to entail the involvement of professional merchants, the more successful of whom came to play a significant role in the politics of their societies and to influence the commercial policies of ancient states. Once the role of trade and traders in ancient economic development has been charted, the key question becomes that of the reasons for antiquity's failure to take the final step and become a fully modern economy:

Why was the victorious advance of capitalism stopped? Why was machinery not invented? Why were the business systems not perfected? Why were the primal forces of primitive economy not overcome? They were gradually disappearing; why did they not disappear completely? To say that they were quantitatively stronger than in our own time does not help us to explain the main phenomenon. (Rostovtzeff 1957: 538)

This view of antiquity can be, and has been, criticised on numerous points. For the 'primitivists', following writers like Weber and Finley, the ancient economy was qualitatively as well as quantitatively different from the modern: not only was there less trade, but it was a different kind of trade, with a different relationship to other areas of society. Classical antiquity was a pre-industrial agrarian society in which the vast majority of the population lived barely above subsistence level; the consequent lack of mass demand, coupled with the high costs of transport, meant that the only goods worth trading were high-value, low-bulk luxuries for the wealthy elite and their dependants (animals for the games clearly fall into this category). Many goods were in fact not traded but 'redistributed' by agents of the state or the nobility; the lioness at Pisa may have been a gift from one aristocrat to another or obtained on commission, rather than being an object of market trade. Traders were poor, dependent, foreign and socially marginalised; ancient states had no discernible commercial policies other than ensuring that they received sufficient food supplies; and trade was always an insignificant part of the economy – even at the height of the Roman Empire one can scarcely imagine many people making a living from transporting lions. The main question from this perspective is not the failure of antiquity to 'take off' into modernity but the lack of any significant economic development; this may be attributed, among other things, to the absence of economic rationality – social status rather than profit was the main goal of human activity – or the dominance of slavery in the economy, or the particular nature of the ancient city as a centre of consumption rather than production.

The problem with this long-running debate – the reason why it has yet to be resolved, and why historians are becoming increasingly frustrated with it (see Morris 1994) – is that the available evidence is inconclusive, because the interpretation of any individual example depends on prior assumptions about the nature of the ancient economy. An example of a trader becoming a member of his city council (*SEG* XVII 828, a 'councillor and shipowner' from Nicomedia in the province of Bithynia, in modern Turkey) can always be proclaimed as the tip of the iceberg, suggesting that there were many others like him whose epitaphs have not survived, or dismissed as an exception. The absence of clear evidence for the involvement of any senatorial families in commerce can be taken at face value as evidence that they did not exist, or explained – with supporting material from early modern Europe – as the natural result of the Roman elite's suspicion of trade: anyone in that position would naturally seek to disguise the commercial origins of the family fortune (D'Arms 1981; cf. Whittaker 1985).

The great advances in archaeology over the last few decades, especially in the analysis of the forms and fabrics of pottery and the excavation of ship-wrecks, and the enormous quantities of material that have been collected and classified, have made surprisingly little difference to this debate (Peacock and Williams 1986; Greene 1997). The ability to identify the points of origin of different pottery containers now makes it impossible to deny that some goods were being moved around at least some areas of the ancient Mediterranean in impressive quantities. Even in the eighth century BCE, for example, 'SOS' amphorae from Attica (named after the decoration that appears on the necks of some of them), probably containing high-quality olive oil, are found in Crete, Cyprus, Sicily, Italy and Spain, while the remains of tens of thousands of Italian Dressel 1 wine amphorae dating to the second and first centuries BCE have been recovered from the River Saône in Gaul (Johnston and Jones 1978; Tchernia 1983). The archaeological perspective is both chronologically and geographically variable, something that is due partly to local conditions of preservation and discovery: a shipwreck is more likely to be noticed – and is easier to excavate – along the south coast of France than off the coast of North Africa, so that shipwreck data are biased towards the north-western Mediterranean, and differences between regions or periods may reflect the nature of the evidence rather than the level of traffic (Parker 1992). Similarly, goods that were transported in more or less indestructible pottery containers are far more visible than perishable goods such as textiles or grain carried in sacks, although it is widely accepted that pottery often rode piggy-back on other cargoes and so can serve as a proxy for other items (see Fulford 1984: 135–6 on grain imports into Roman Britain). The movement of livestock, whether animals or human slaves, is almost completely invisible. For all these uncertainties, however, archaeological evidence is far more copious and far less susceptible to bias than anything to be found in the literary sources.

The problem arises when one tries to go beyond acknowledging the existence of inter-regional connections and the widespread distribution of goods to assess their economic significance. Briefly, archaeology shows that goods are being moved, but rarely by whom, or in what context. No historian would now follow Finley's wholesale rejection of archaeological evidence, on the basis of the fact that thirty-nine sherds of *terra sigillata* scattered over a 400-metre area on the Swedish island of Gotland were eventually found to belong to the same bowl (1999: 33), but it is difficult to refute Whittaker's equally sceptical argument that the distribution of wine amphorae in the Roman period might simply represent aristocrats moving their own produce between different estates rather than market trade (1989). Such redistributive practices are certainly recorded and conform better to what we know of ancient values and ideology than does market trade; modernisers of course reply that the literary sources which disparage trade are the product of the landed elite and cannot be assumed to be representative of all sectors of society. Tens of thousands of pottery sherds confirm their belief in the high development of ancient commerce, but they are insufficient to dismiss the arguments of the primitivists as to why trade could not have been large-scale or economically significant in a pre-industrial society with limited demand (Tchernia 1989).

TRADE AND MODERNITY

Despite the unbridgeable differences in their perspectives on what antiquity was like, which are often reinforced by very different conceptions about how it should be studied, primitivists and modernisers do share a number of important assumptions. In the first place, there is now general agreement that antiquity was predominantly an agrarian society, even if disagreement remains on the significance of this point. As Cartledge puts it:

Primitivists tend to be trying to explain how the 98% of Greeks 'economized', that is, secured a bare livelihood within the framework of the ideally (yet rarely) self-sufficient *oikos* or household; whereas the modernizers focus instead on the 2% of exceptions for whom macro-economic activity at a regional or international level was the sole or primary source of their wealth. (1998: 6)

However, this is not simply a matter of emphasis and scholarly preference; rather, it is central to what both sides regard as the crucial question, whether antiquity should be considered 'modern' or 'not-modern'. This approach rests on a number of related assumptions, each of which is also found in modern discussions of economic structures and in particular in discussions of 'economic development' in the Third World (see Hill 1986). The first is that this dichotomy is indeed the right way to think about economic systems: the industrialised, capitalist West represents the only feasible model for successful economic development, so that the choice is between 'modernity' along western lines and non-modern stagnation. Secondly, it is assumed that the modernity of an economy should be understood primarily in terms of the place of trade within it, rather than in terms of, say, production or patterns of consumption. 'In order to understand the ancient economy, we need to know the part played in it by trade and traders' (Hopkins 1983a: ix); when western governments and financial institutions advise Third World countries on 'modernisation' – or attach conditions to financial aid packages – these invariably involve shifting production towards marketable goods rather than subsistence crops and the removal of restrictions on the market (see Stiglitz 2002). Trade is regarded as a natural human impulse, so that its development is assumed to be inevitable once 'impediments' are removed. In considering pre-modern societies, what is assumed to matter is their resemblance to a particular version of the history of the emergence of the modern economy, in which trade is given a central role.

According to this account, which owes a great deal to Max Weber, trade played a crucial role in the emergence of the late medieval city as a politically independent institution; the separation of town and country then fostered the development of a distinctive mentality emphasising rational decision-making and valuing the accumulation of wealth, and the emergence of a new class of men who put this into practice through their entrepreneurial activities (Weber 1958; Braudel 1982; a critique in Holton 1986). The imperatives of trade and the capitalist mentality then drove the European expansion across the globe in search of new and cheaper sources of merchandise and, increasingly, new markets for the products of Europe; it underpinned the Industrial Revolution as the mediator between demand and supply, providing the incentive for innovation and investment; it continues to be the lifeblood of the world economy, supporting the global division of labour that ensures that resources are exploited as efficiently as possible (see Wallerstein 1974, 1980).

Many elements of this account have been questioned, but that is beside the point; this version remains the yardstick against which antiquity is regularly, if often only implicitly, measured in the primitivist–modernising dispute. This implicit comparison not only explains the prominence of trade in the argument, but also some of the particular (if not peculiar) characteristics of the way that trade is discussed. For example, the question of whether aristocrats were involved in trade or whether traders ever joined the political elite may appear tangential to arguments about the economic importance of ancient trade, but it is driven by a comparison with the late medieval trading cities of the Hanseatic League, ruled by merchant families and hence, according to Weber, the breeding grounds of the 'Protestant ethic' that drove the development of capitalism (1992). On the basis of this historical comparison, modernisers like Rostovtzeff tend to assume without question that traders will develop and promulgate their own set of bourgeois values; primitivists, on the other hand, downplay the significance of trade because there is little trace in antiquity of any alternative ideology to that of the landed elite. Unless the wider intellectual context is taken into account, both arguments seem largely beside the point. The same can be said of the debate about whether ancient cities were centres of consumption or production, or about the existence of a narrowly defined 'economic rationalism'; vital questions if one assumes that the choice lies only between 'modern' and 'not-modern' and that later medieval and early modern Europe are the only valid models of developing modernity, but otherwise a distraction from more productive questions.

The third assumption underlying this debate, which does not always sit comfortably with the second, is that 'trade' needs to be understood in terms of the modern ideal – driven solely by the profit motive and market forces, unfettered by social or political constraints, encompassing every aspect of material existence – rather than any historical or contemporary reality. This leads both modernisers and primitivists to build arguments around some allegedly clear distinctions, the implications of which are unexamined and taken for granted: public and private, luxury and staple, self-sufficiency and economic rationality. For example, as will be discussed in more detail in chapter 3, it is simply assumed that only trade in staple goods had real economic significance; luxury trade is regarded as intrinsically superfluous and trivial, despite the importance of non-essential items such as spices, tea and sugar in the development of trade in the early modern period. Only pure profit maximisation is accepted as economically rational, so that self-sufficiency (which may be a perfectly rational strategy) is dismissed as unproductive; the involvement of the state in any activity is assumed automatically to work against the possibility of proper economic development. Perhaps the most problematic distinction is that between the economic and the social; it is certainly a valid criticism of modernising approaches that 'the economy' was not an entirely separate sphere of human activity in antiquity (see Finley 1999: 17–34) – but this is equally true of the present day. The fact that ancient trade was influenced by concerns with social status and other cultural factors does not mean that it was therefore not really an economic activity.

One of the aims of this book is to explore and break down some of these distinctions, and to identify what distinguished trade in classical antiquity not only from the modern world but from other pre-modern societies. The contrast between ancient and modern represents one way of identifying issues that may need to be addressed, but it is not an end in itself. Rather as the World Bank refuses to consider whether alternative approaches to economic management might be more appropriate in some cases than their doctrine of free trade (bearing in mind that most western countries followed wholeheartedly protectionist policies while they were building their industrial bases: Madeley 2000; Stiglitz 2002), so ancient historians have tended to fall into a dichotomy of modernity or stagnation, rather than considering whether different pre-modern societies might have their own dynamics of development and laws of motion. The primitivists are clearly correct in their insistence on the need to understand ancient trade in the context of a pre-industrial, predominantly agrarian society with limited technical resources and strict limits on the possibility of increasing surplus production (Wrigley 1988). However, the modernisers are right to focus on the 2 per cent of activity that was not wholly devoted to subsistence: the ways in which the surplus production of ancient society was mobilised, managed and consumed – including the role of trade and traders – is one of the key things that distinguishes antiquity from other pre-industrial agrarian societies. To consider trading activity simply as a 'veneer' on the vast mass of subsistence-orientated activity begs the question: would classical antiquity have taken the same form and developed in the same manner if there had been no system for the widespread distribution of material goods?

DEFINITIONS

However, this does itself beg a further question, insofar as so much of the primitivist–modernising debate involves arguments about which activities can appropriately be labelled 'trade'. Trade is clearly a form of exchange, in which goods are passed from one person to another, but it is not the only form. Anthropologists have distinguished between reciprocity, redistribution and market exchange (trade) as different modes for the distribution of goods within a society (Polanyi 1957); one of the most important contributions of the primitivist school has been to emphasise the crucial role played by both reciprocity (the exchange of gifts) and redistribution (whether by powerful individuals or by states) in the ancient economy, where the modernisers tended to regard any form of exchange as trade. However, too narrow a definition of trade can be as misleading as an excessively broad one; if the label 'trade' is, for example, restricted to 'the purchase and movement of goods without the knowledge or identification of a further purchaser' (Snodgrass 1983: 26) then it was indeed a rare phenomenon through much of antiquity – but is it correct to insist that only the activities of independent professional traders should count as 'trade', excluding the case of a farmer like Hesiod transporting his own goods to market (*Works and Days* 618–94)? At the other end of the scale, is there a meaningful distinction to be drawn – presumably on the basis of scale of activity – between 'trade' and 'commerce'?

For some purposes, such distinctions are extremely important. The cultural meaning of exchange from the perspective of the actors involved is usually affected by the 'social distance' between them – that is, the Greeks and Romans did regard gift exchange between friends as clearly different from obtaining goods through the market, even if in practice the distinction was not always clear-cut (Sahlins 1972; von Reden 1995a: 2–3). The extent to which exchange activities in a given society involved some full-time specialist traders can be an important indicator of their degree of development. In other instances, however, the distinction between market trade and other forms of exchange may be less significant. In an agrarian economy with high transport costs, evidence for the movement of any goods over significant distances, through whatever mechanisms, is interesting, raising questions about the way that this portion of the agricultural surplus is being deployed and about the implications of the development of 'connectivity'. The environmental structures that create conditions of scarcity and the uneven distribution of resources, thus creating a need for exchange, are common to the different forms of exchange that are developed; so too the patterns of consumption and desire that determine the value of the objects involved. For much of this book, I shall be considering the broad subject of 'distribution', encompassing all the different ways in which this may be managed; later chapters will pay more attention to the distinction between trade and other forms of exchange – above all because this distinction mattered to the ancients themselves, which in turn affected the actual practices of exchange.

A similar point can be made about the question of physical distance. 'Trade' is sometimes glossed as 'inter-regional trade', to distinguish it from smaller-scale local exchange. For some purposes this is significant, not least because long-distance trade requires a greater investment of resources in distribution, something that both requires an explanation and is likely to have social and economic consequences. However, the distinction between short- and long-distance distribution will always be somewhat arbitrary; so too the definition of a 'region', since in some instances political boundaries and in others ecological considerations will carry the most weight. It seems preferable to conceive of the ancient world in terms of overlapping spheres of exchange, as the boundaries between different eco-systems came to be overlaid with political boundaries that partially reshaped patterns of distribution, and to see different exchange practices as part of a spectrum in terms of both distance and scale. Trade may be considered in the broadest sense as the movement of goods across different sorts of boundaries: household, tribe, state, status, ecological. The Greek peasant carrying his surplus produce to the local town market is doing something that is different, but not absolutely distinct, from the merchant shipping grain between Egypt and Athens; for the most part, their activities need to be understood through the same set of analytical tools and concepts.

APPROACHES

Running in parallel and intersecting with the primitivist–modernising debate – often, it must be said, with confusing results – is the dispute between substantivism and formalism, about how pre-modern economies should be studied (Morley 2004: 43–5). Formalists assume that the principles and practices of neoclassical economic theory are universally valid and applicable; substantivists argue that they are valid only for the modern capitalist economy, since they ignore the extent to which pre-modern economies were 'embedded' in society rather than being distinct spheres of activity. The application of modern economic categories and concepts is tantamount to 'modernising' the ancient economy, scarcely distinguishable from Rostovtzeff's unselfconscious use of the term 'bourgeoisie' to describe the traders of the Hellenistic cities; substantivists turn instead to alternative conceptual schemes, such as the anthropological distinction between reciprocity, redistribution and market exchange.

This argument rests on a certain misunderstanding of the purpose and status of an economic model (Morris 2001). It is not intended as an accurate description of the real world but as a kind of utopia, a thought experiment based on deliberately simplifying assumptions: how would key variables – at the simplest level, say, supply, demand and price – interact if there were no other factors involved? It must be admitted that some economists can behave as if their theories and categories are both universal and normative, ignoring the extent to which they are based on wholly unrealistic assumptions, and so the hostile reaction of ancient historians is understandable, but this is not intrinsic to economic theory. Its basic principles underlie the analysis of trade offered here.

If this book does not appear particularly 'economic' in its style, it is because many of the simplifying assumptions of economic theory, such as perfect information, pure economic rationality and frictionless markets, are even less realistic for classical antiquity than they are for the modern world. Further, we simply lack the detailed evidence for changes in supply, demand and price of any good, let alone the market as a whole, to construct a sufficiently detailed model of the ancient economy for the application of economic analysis. We can follow the example of Hopkins in producing abstract models based on 'orders of magnitude' (e.g. 1980; 1995/6) to identify some of the underlying processes of economic change, but even this approach has its limits. A margin of error of 10 per cent (even that is perhaps optimistic) is acceptable in a discussion of the population of Rome or the gross domestic product of the Roman Empire, whereas for Athens that would constitute the basis for radically different views of population and the need for imported grain (Morris 1994). One might attempt to construct a larger model of 'the Greek world', but that would be undermined by the fact that so much of the evidence relates to the exceptional case of Athens, and by our knowledge of the likely economic effects of political fragmentation. In analysing the ancient economy, the most important use of economic models is in identifying issues that are worth exploring, which are precisely those points where the model clearly diverges from historical reality (North 1981; Morris 2001). Neoclassical economics indicates what would be the most efficient distribution of a given set of resources under conditions of scarcity, all other things being equal; we turn to the insights offered by other disciplines as to why resources ended up being distributed rather differently.

The next two chapters take a step back from the starting assumptions of economic theory to explore the origins and parameters of demand. Both the scarcity and the non-uniform distribution of vital resources in classical antiquity derive from the environmental structures of northern Europe and the Mediterranean region. As recent studies of the ecology of the Mediterranean have suggested, the environment can be both an impediment and a stimulus to trade. Exchange is one way (but by no means the only way) both of gaining access to resources that are more abundant in another region and of responding to the conditions of risk and uncertainty that are endemic to agrarian economics in general and, according to Horden and Purcell's monumental study, to the Mediterranean in particular (2000); on the other hand, the topography of the different regions shapes, directs and hinders the movement of both people and material objects. The aim of chapter 2 is to identify the physical structures that conditioned human activity: the 'limits of the possible', in Braudel's phrase (1981: 27), which could be breached but only at a high cost in terms of effort and resources.

By the classical period, lions were not generally to be found in Europe; any demand for them could be met only through some sort of distributive system. However, lions are not always regarded as potential objects of trade and do not seem to have been treated as such before the Roman period; a market for wild, non-edible beasts exists only in certain cultural contexts. Chapter 3 considers the origins of demand by focusing on the development of patterns of consumption. Anthropological and sociological approaches have long argued that the importance of the objects of trade is not reducible to their economic value; the consumption of particular objects in particular ways may serve to legitimise political structures, establish claims to social status or identify the consumer's social identity and adherence to a given set of values. The introduction of lavish spectacles, gladiatorial combats and wild-beast shows as part of the funerals of elite Romans, conditioned by the need to compete with one's rivals for political power and resting on an ideology that valued triumphing over nature and controlling the exotic, created a demand for lions (Wiedemann 1992). The importance of such goods for Roman society is seen in their role in aristocratic competition and display, not just their contribution to gross domestic product. The demand for apparently 'natural' commodities like grain and wine equally needs to be understood in social and cultural terms – and not simply according to the categories of 'luxury' and 'staple' that are commonly used in the study of the objects of ancient trade.

The following two chapters focus on the social and psychological structures that shaped the practices of exchange and distribution. Neoclassical economic theory traditionally ignores the role of social institutions in exchange; transactions are assumed to take place effortlessly and without any costs. The New Institutional Economics, a recent school of economic history, argues that, on the contrary, exchange is barely conceivable without social institutions to constrain and condition human behaviour (North 1981, 1990; Morris 2001). Exchange requires agreement between the two parties, and thus some basis for agreement, whether in terms of the measurement of the quantitative and qualitative attributes of the objects of exchange or in terms of the establishment and enforcement of the conditions of exchange. Institutions provide such structures; in antiquity this means, above all, the institutions of the state, as the enforcer and creator of laws and the source and guarantor of measures and money. However, the ancient state was never simply the passive facilitator of exchange: it intervened regularly and significantly – mobilising and redistributing resources, encouraging or regulating the activities of traders, above all seeking to protect its own interests and pursue its own goals – in ways that directly affected the structures of ancient trade. Non-state institutions, too, played a part, in the financing and management of overseas expeditions, and the nature of the structures developed in antiquity shaped and, arguably, limited the development of systems of distribution. The wreck at Pisa cannot answer questions about ownership or the financing of trade – but it immediately points to the potential importance of some form of insurance, as provided in the way that ancient maritime loans were organised, in limiting the risks involved in such ventures.

Chapter 5 turns from formal to informal institutions: the attitudes, beliefs and value systems that shaped individuals' economic behaviour. Ancient exchange practices were indeed 'embedded' in social structures and affected by the development of traditions of thought that regarded both trade and traders with hostility. The objects of trade, too, and the ways in which they were consumed could become the focus of moral and political debate, as in the ancient discourse on 'luxury' (which might include excessively lavish and exotic funeral games), and this in turn reflected on the people and practices that introduced such problematic objects into society. However, the lack of separation between the social and the economic works both ways: ideas about exchange come to offer a template for conceptualising social relations, and in debates about the limits of self-sufficiency, the morality of particular forms of consumption and the commoditisation of objects, the economic, social and political become inextricably entwined. The disparaging attitude of many ancient sources towards trade and traders, frequently blamed for the limited economic development of antiquity, is often a strategy of self-positioning in relation to a set of ideals and values – whether that of the true aristocrat, the good citizen, the traditionally minded Roman or the faithful Christian.

The aim of this book is not to offer a chronological history of the development of trade and commerce or to draw up lists of the goods that were traded between regions, but to identify the different structures – physical, social, ideological – that shaped the distribution of goods and the practices of exchange across the ancient world. However, it must not be forgotten that such structures change over time, as a result of human action as well as external pressures. This is true even of the apparently unchanging structures of the environment, as patterns of cultivation change with the introduction of new crops and techniques, or as the exploitation of resources leads to their degradation or exhaustion; it is obviously true of more malleable structures like political institutions, attitudes and taste. There are times, therefore, when a particular theme can usefully be illustrated with sources from the whole span of classical antiquity; at other times, we need to be alert to the variations between different periods and cultures.

'The ancient economy' is rarely a helpful concept, since it tends to look uniform only in so far as it is contrasted with modernity. It does not necessarily help, however, to replace it with smaller chronological divisions like 'the Athenian', 'the Hellenistic' or 'the late Roman' economy; the different structures that shaped ancient trade did not change at the same pace, so that any attempt at defining periods of economic development will invariably involve arbitrary distinctions based on one set of criteria (usually, the historical divisions of traditional political history) at the expense of others. The aim of the final chapter is to consider how far there may indeed have developed 'an economy' at any period of classical antiquity, in the sense of a relatively integrated and interacting sphere of activity uniting more than one region. In recent years various theoretical approaches have attempted to consider historical developments at a global level and to identify the underlying determinants of change; a reflection, undoubtedly, of the sense that we are living in an increasingly interconnected and interdependent world. How far this was true of antiquity, or whether it was rather a world of more or less independent, only loosely connected cells, is the main question here. One thing is clear, that trade was not an autonomous force of globalisation; it was closely connected to, and frequently dependent upon, the integrative force of imperialism.

Lastly, this chapter will consider the limits to ancient connectivity, and the relationship between changes in the structures of trade and exchange and the gradual disintegration – taking that term literally, as a process of loosened ties and reduced communication – of the Roman Empire. In the early medieval period, trade was indeed something of a veneer on a predominantly agrarian society, scarcely touching the lives of the majority of the population (McCormick 2001). This development calls for consideration of how far connectivity and interdependence may have costs and drawbacks as well as benefits for a society, and how far this may have accelerated the move towards a less connected world.

How, then, do the Pisa wreck and its cargo fit into a new account of trade in classical antiquity? They stand for the development of connectivity across the Mediterranean, with the movement of people, goods and information; for the development of the technology, infrastructure and institutions that underpinned and encouraged such movement; and, given the fate of the ship, for the risks and uncertainty that characterised any such venture. It is impossible to say anything useful about the frequency of this sort of traffic, how far it may have made how many people wealthy, and whether this wreck would have brought about somebody's ruin – but its importance is not to be understood in purely financial terms. As argued above, trade in lions has to be understood in the context of Roman aristocratic competition, expressed first and foremost in the sheer numbers of animals being slaughtered – and hence an increase in demand for them – but also in the search for ever more exotic creatures for the arena. The foreign origin of the object of trade is not simply a reflection of the geographical distribution of lions in the ancient Mediterranean but is part of its meaning and its appeal; so too the range of qualities that come to be ascribed to lions in literature and visual representations (see Toynbee 1973: 61–9). At the same time, the object and the process that brought it to Italy become implicated in debates about the proper limits of aristocratic competitiveness and the social consequences of their spending, expressed in the language of 'luxury' as excessive or inappropriate consumption of particular commodities (Edwards 1993). The development of trade and distribution depended on, but also made possible, the structures and institutions of ancient society; Rome would have looked rather different without lions.

CHAPTER 2

Ecology and economics

Suppose that there is a time of dearth and famine at Rhodes, with provisions being sold at fabulous prices; and suppose that an honest man has imported a large cargo of grain from Alexandria and that to his certain knowledge several other importers have set sail from Alexandria, and that in the course of the voyage he has sighted their vessels laden with grain and headed for Rhodes; is he bound to report this fact to the people of Rhodes, or is he to keep his own counsel and sell his goods at the highest market price?

(Cic. *Off.* 3.50)

From today's perspective, the fact that Cicero can consider that such a situation would ever present a merchant with a moral dilemma seems to epitomise the distance between ancient and modern economic mentality. His stress on the honesty of the man, given the views that he expresses about traders earlier in the same work (1.150–1), is significant; in so far as this thought experiment relates to actual behaviour, it is that of the young Roman noble rather than any merchant. However, the situation in which such a dilemma *ought* to exist is intended to be believable: it exemplifies not only the ubiquity of food crisis (not necessarily famine: Garnsey 1988: 17–39) and the reliance on imports of grain, but the slowness of transport, the scarcity of information and the volatility of the market. Classical antiquity, like other pre-modern societies, was a world of uncertainty and vulnerability; trade arose from these conditions and was shaped by them, sometimes relieving and sometimes contributing to the insecurity of everyday life.

MODES OF ACCUMULATION

In recent years a number of studies have emphasised the importance of studying ancient history in relation to the environment: physical topography, climate, flora and fauna are not simply the scenic backdrop to historical events but help to shape their course and influence – if not determine – their outcome (Cartledge 1979; Sallares 1991; Horden and Purcell 2000). This is most obvious in considering the ways in which humans obtain their basic material needs: the interaction between the dynamics of the human population and those of other populations, including food crops, animals and pathogenic micro-organisms, which is shaped by the particular conditions and resources of the ecosystem, affects such vital factors as the size of the population, its life expectancy and its nutritional status, with direct consequences for social structure, military capability, the workings of politics, and so forth.

In ecological terms, one of the striking things about humans is their ability to overcome some environmental constraints, and even to modify their environment, through the use of technology. For most animal and plant populations, the availability of resources in the ecosystem sets limits on their capacity for expansion; when this limit is reached, it is necessary either to limit population growth or, if possible, to move to another area. Humans have at times followed similar strategies – the phenomenon of Greek colonisation is now commonly interpreted as at least in part a response to relative overpopulation – but they have also developed alternative techniques: clearing more ground for farming, the introduction of new crops or new farming methods, and the acquisition of resources from outside the region (Sallares 1991: 73–84). The last technique includes, but is not limited to, trade; war, banditry and piracy might be equally effective modes of accumulation. Thucydides' speculative reconstruction of the history of early Greece first imagines a world 'without trade and without freedom of communication by either land or sea' (1.2.1) and then, 'as communication by sea became more common', one where piracy was ubiquitous (1.5). The 'Homeric' *Hymn to Apollo*, probably dating to the sixth century BCE, expresses the concern that seafaring strangers might equally be pirates as traders (452–5), and the evidence suggests that piracy remained a problem throughout antiquity, increasingly parasitic on distributive activities, despite the claims of various states to have brought it under control (de Souza 1999).

War, piracy and trade all involve the expenditure of energy in the process of acquisition, in producing the necessary equipment (ships, goods for exchange or weapons) and in travelling, and presuppose the existence of an agricultural surplus. One can only speculate about the grounds on which one strategy was adopted rather than another: the potential gains from piracy were considerable, as there was no need to hand over goods in return, but so were the potential risks; trade was more efficient in so far as it required the involvement of fewer people, and less hazardous for the individual. It also offered a better prospect of repeat transactions and a more regular supply of necessary resources, especially those which were not common in a region. Even in the violent world of the Homeric poems there were traders, regarded as the obvious sources of more specialised goods like metals (e.g. *Il.* 7.467–75). The importance of violence as a mode of accumulation and a cultural practice in antiquity can scarcely be exaggerated, but it is clear that as early as the eighth century BCE much, if not most, of the task of remedying the deficiencies in a particular region was assigned to more peaceful forms of redistribution. The early Greek overseas settlements may not, as was once thought, have been founded for the purposes of trade, but they undoubtedly drew on the knowledge of prior peaceful contacts with the regions to which they were sent, and they assumed that there would be sufficient visits in future to maintain links with the homeland (Snodgrass 1980; Osborne forthcoming).

UBIQUITY AND VARIETY

In ecological terms, therefore, systems of distribution represent one way in which the 'limits of the possible' in a particular ecosystem can be exceeded through the expenditure of time and resources. The next question is how far the characteristics of the environments of the classical world may have affected the development of such systems. Interestingly, it has been argued both that they represented a strong impediment to the development of trade and that they would have promoted a high level of connectivity and distributive activity, both 'high commerce' between regions and a constant background noise of the short-haul coastal trading known as *cabotage* (Horden and Purcell 2000: 124–72).

The first line of argument emphasises the homogeneity of the Mediterranean environment and of the way in which it was exploited. The basic components of the ancient diet – grain, wine, olive oil – were ubiquitous. No region could develop any comparative advantage in their production – that is to say, produce them so much more cheaply or efficiently than other regions that they could undercut local products once the costs of transport were taken into account – so there was no basis for their exchange. Individual cities and regions focused instead on ensuring their own self-sufficiency, since they could scarcely count on supplies from elsewhere. The same was true for other products: the raw materials, such as wool, clay or wood, were found everywhere and were expensive to transport over long distances, and the techniques for working them were rudimentary and ubiquitous. Surplus production was limited, so that the mass of the population had little capacity to consume non-subsistence items and few areas could afford to become reliant on regular imports. The result was that there is no trace in antiquity of the development of regional specialisation, like the vast herds of sheep of medieval East Anglia or the pottery industry of seventeenth-century Delft; goods were consumed locally, predominantly by their producers, while only a few high-value items for the wealthy elites were ever distributed more widely.

As always, the 'primitivist' perspective on the ancient economy rests on a potentially misleading contrast with modernity: the fact that there was indeed no regional specialisation in antiquity on the scale of, say, the grain fields of the American Midwest does not mean that there was no trade of any significance. A closer examination of the structures of the environment suggests a number of ways in which the picture of absolute homogeneity is overdrawn. Certainly it is not the image that ancient writers had of their own world. The practical impossibility of self-sufficiency and hence the need for regular imports were acknowledged even by those who might have preferred to do without the corrupting influence of foreign trade: 'It is almost impossible to found a state in a place where it will not need imports' (Plato, *Rep.* 370e; cf. Arist. *Pol.* 1327a). In Aristophanes' *Acharnians*, the basic principle of exchange is to obtain 'something we don't have at home but is plentiful around here' (900) – even if Attica's only desirable export for the moment is 'an informer, packed up like crockery' (904). For the compilers of geographical surveys in the Roman period, such as Strabo or the Elder Pliny or the fourth-century *Expositio Totius Mundi*, regions were defined by the uniqueness or abundance of their products and their capacity for exporting them (e.g. Strabo 3.2.4–6; Pliny, *NH* 37.202–3). For a Christian preacher in the fourth century, God's creation was the very opposite of homogeneous and free from trade: 'God filled the earth with goods but gave each region its own particular products, so that, moved by need, we would communicate and share among ourselves, giving others that of which we have abundance and receiving that which we lack' (John Chrysostom, *Hom. de perfecta caritate* 1).

The homogeneity of the Mediterranean environment depends on the scale at which you consider it. It is perfectly true that Greece, Italy, southern France and Spain have broadly similar climates, soils and terrain and grow the same sorts of crops – above all, the Mediterranean triad of wheat, vines and olives (King, Proudfoot and Smith 1997). However, not all parts of these countries could produce all these crops. Vines and olives are temperature-sensitive and can be grown successfully only up to a certain altitude; olives are particularly fussy, requiring both a dry summer and cool but frost-free winter (Tchernia 1986; Sallares 1991: 304–90). Grain crops, particularly wheat, are more productive and less likely to fail down in the valleys (Garnsey 1988: 9–10). The original historian of the Mediterranean environment, Fernand Braudel, argued that there was a fundamental distinction between mountains, hills and plains in environmental conditions and hence in economic structures (1972: 25–102). Some individuals might move between these different zones, keeping flocks in the hills in summer and on their valley farms (where they contributed manure) in winter. In many cases, however, the pastoral and arable economies grew apart, developing a mutual suspicion – shepherds were commonly associated with banditry – but connected by the possibility of exchanging wool and meat for oil and wine (Shaw 1984; Whittaker 1988; Grünewald 2004). In Strabo's account the Ligurians of northern Italy subsist on the produce of their herds and a drink made from barley, but trade wool, cattle, hides and honey for the oil and wine of Italy (4.6.2). Coastal regions, wooded areas and even apparently barren scrubland and desert had their own specialities: fish, salt and salted fish, and wild game of all kinds.

Even the valleys and plains of the Mediterranean were not homogeneous, except in contrast to the hill country. One indicator of the existence of variation is the way that certain regions became renowned in antiquity for the production of grain. Egypt, with the benefit of the annual Nile flood, was exceptional – to the extent that its status as a 'Mediterranean' region, according to any of the usual criteria, is seriously in doubt (Bagnall 2005). Other, less atypical, regions also enjoyed more favourable growing conditions than others: the Black Sea region, Sicily, North Africa, Campania – 'the land is in crop all year round!' (Pliny, *NH* 18.111) – compared with Apulia or Bruttium, and the Argive plain compared with Attica. The production of a substantial marketable surplus of course depends on more than a marginal advantage in soil fertility or the reliability of rainfall – demography, social structures and political institutions are equally influential – but it was clearly easier to achieve this in some areas than others. Even minor differences in soil, relief, climate and the availability of water can make a considerable difference to agricultural yields, and it is argued strongly that, if 'the Mediterranean' has any clear identity, it lies not in any homogeneous characteristics but in the degree of fragmentation and variation, a kind of 'unity in diversity', with significant differences in ecological conditions even between adjacent valleys (Horden and Purcell 2000: 53–88).

The final point to note is that the classical world was not completely isolated from its neighbours, and was not always confined to the

Mediterranean; it not only bordered on regions with quite different ecosystems and products but frequently encompassed them (Harris 2005b: 21–9). The south of France broadly fits the conventional pattern of Mediterranean terrain and climate, with the caveats noted above, so for much of antiquity it produced a similar range of crops to Italy and Spain, but climate and soil alike change as one heads further north. Olive oil, a central component of the ancient diet and of cultural practices like bathing, would always have to be imported into northern areas, or substituted with animal fats, but these regions were better suited to animal husbandry – to the extent that the excessive consumption of meat and milk became, for classical writers, one of the key characteristics of the stereotypical barbarian (Garnsey 1999: 66–8). The East, meanwhile, was equally strongly associated with its distinctive products such as spices, silk and incense, obtainable only through some form of redistribution or exchange. The Hellenistic empires brought together regions with different ecological conditions and products, enhancing the possibility of exchange between them; so too the Roman Empire. 'Who would not admit', argued the Elder Pliny, 'that now that communication has been established through the whole world by the power of the Roman Empire . . . even things that had previously been hidden have all now been established in general use' (*NH* 14.2).

The environment was not homogeneous; nor were its products, either in quantity, as noted above, or in quality. The differences might be relatively small or even entirely negligible in terms of the functional qualities of the objects – the nutritional value of foodstuffs, for example, or the warmth provided by a woollen tunic – but they could be immensely important in terms of the development of patterns of consumption. For example, the quality of wine from different regions varies dramatically, even in the modern era of industrialised viticulture, depending not only on the varieties grown and the production techniques but on subtle differences in the mineral content of the soil, the nature of the terrain and the levels of sunlight and rainfall during the growing season (Tchernia 1986). From a very early date a certain proportion of consumption moved from undifferentiated 'wine' to wines identified by their place of origin; even in Homer guests may be offered 'Pramnian' wine (*Il.* 11.639; *Od.* 10.235). By the first century CE the Elder Pliny is expressing his astonishment that Virgil had listed only fifteen different kinds of grape, and insisting that what distinguishes different wines is not the grape but the country and the soil (*NH* 14.7, 70). In many regions one wine might be produced for local mass consumption and another for special occasions and export (the Roman ideal became a wine that would somehow combine quality *and* quantity: Tchernia 1986:

211–14). The arguments that Pliny records about the claims to superiority of different varieties suggest that such products were not considered interchangeable; a wine-producing region might still import wines from other areas. This was a specialised sector of the wine trade and limited in volume if not necessarily in profitability; but it is part of a wider pattern in which environmental differences and specialised local products go hand in hand with the development of discriminating taste and a preference for the exotic.

> Just like the products of India, or silk from Persia, or all the things that are grown and harvested in the land of the Ethiopians but are carried everywhere by the custom of trade, so, too, our native fig does not grow anywhere else on earth, but is exported by us to every part of it. (Ps.-Julian, *Ep.* 80: 'On the Damascus fig')

Wool could be found in every region, but here too the compilers of encyclopaedias could identify numerous differences and gradations in quality, colour and suitability for particular purposes, all based on regional differences as much as on breeds of sheep – in some cases, a distinctive colour had no name other than the place of origin of the wool (Pliny, *NH* 8.190–3). Such lists can be multiplied for other products. In most cases, of course, and certainly the further we move from the archaic period, the distinctions are not based purely on environmental differences; they reflect also the choices made by the inhabitants of different regions as to how best to exploit their environment, influenced by the existence of a market for distinctive products as much as they made such a trade possible. This was also the case with some manufactured products: the basic techniques of producing pottery were more or less universal, but the ability to produce certain forms and fabrics – red-glazed *terra sigillata*, for example – was geographically restricted and so created the possibility for inter-regional exchange, at least until the technique was communicated or copied (Woolf 1997: 169–205). The development of distinctive patterns of decoration created the possibility of the profitable exchange of otherwise ubiquitous, low-value and utilitarian objects (see Gill 1991, 1994; Osborne 1996).

The raw materials for pottery were widely, if not absolutely uniformly, distributed; other mineral resources were not. The most obvious examples are metals, and not only precious metals. These come to be closely associated with the particular regions where they were abundant and/or easily extracted; from a very early date they become the objects of redistribution, as seen in descriptions of Phoenician merchant activities and the copper ingots found in bronze-age shipwrecks such as that found off Cape Gelidonya in south-west Turkey (Parker 1992: 108–9). Iron and lead were relatively ubiquitous – that is to say, they could be found in most regions, but by no means every part of them – but copper, silver, gold and tin were far rarer (Healy 1978, 45–67). As Strabo remarked: 'The whole country of the Iberians is full of metals, although not all of it is so rich in fruit, or so fertile either . . . It is rare for a country to be fortunate in both respects, and it is also rare for the same country to have within a small area an abundance of all kinds of metals' (3.2.8). The Phoenicians, it has been suggested, made their fortunes by connecting worlds where precious metals had different values because of their relative abundance or scarcity (Moscati 1968: 180), and certainly most of the early evidence for Phoenician and Greek activity in the western Mediterranean is found in the vicinity of sources of metals, in Italy, Sardinia and Spain. Stone suitable for building was not found everywhere, especially not high-quality decorative marbles, but the same can be said of some far less valuable and exotic but equally essential objects: the storage of many agricultural crops, for example, depended on obtaining supplies of pitch to line barrels and jars, and often large quantities of salt for preserving.

The ancient environment was not homogeneous at any time – and certainly not homogeneous over time. In the first place, crops were not grown everywhere at all periods. Vines can potentially be grown through most of the Mediterranean, but their introduction into different regions by Greeks, Phoenicians and Romans can be roughly charted from the eighth century BCE, when Greek wine containers first appear in Italy, to the first two centuries CE, when Spain and Gaul began to export their own wine back to Rome as well as consuming Italian products. The diffusion of olive cultivation was similarly gradual; meanwhile, grain may have been ubiquitous but the varieties grown in different areas, not only wheat as opposed to barley but different varieties of wheat, suited to particular uses, changed significantly over time, in response to changing techniques of processing and new patterns of consumption (Sallares 1991: 14–18). That is to say, any region could supply some sort of grain for its population, but, at least until the middle Principate, a demand for high-quality bread wheat would in many areas have to be supplied through some form of long-distance redistribution.

Secondly, there was considerable variation in the short term: the climate in most regions and microregions of the Mediterranean can fluctuate dramatically from year to year, especially in the level of rainfall, so harvests tend to lurch between glut and dearth rather than offering steady and predictable yields. Periodic harvest failure and food crisis seem to have been the norm in antiquity, interspersed with the enjoyment of windfall surpluses

(Garnsey 1988; cf. Olshausen and Sonnabend 1998). Redistribution was not the only means by which short-term shortages could be remedied: individual farmers might hope to rely on storage facilities, cultivation techniques – including taking advantage of local microecologies by dispersing holdings across a wide area – and family and other relationships (Garnsey 1988: 43–68). Non-producers, above all in the cities, were in any case dependent on the market for their sustenance, so had to hope that it would now draw in supplies from outside the region as well as from the local countryside, perhaps assisted by the generosity of the local elite. For those regions with a surplus, trade was not the only option either, but the potential gains from redistribution, whether sending grain as a gift or selling it to merchants, were normally greater than simply consuming it locally. Hopkins' outline model of this process suggests that, in any given year under the Roman Empire, a minimum of nearly half a million tonnes of grain would have to be redistributed to compensate for local shortfalls, cargoes worth over 200 million sesterces (1983b).

Discussion of interannual variations in yield has tended to focus on grain as the basic and more or less indispensable foodstuff of antiquity, but the variations affected other crops as well. The Younger Pliny discusses the problems of the wine merchants who had bid for a share of his grape harvest in advance and had then been disappointed by the results, failing to recoup their investments; the laws concerning the sale of 'grapes on the vine' were debated extensively among Roman lawyers because, given the unpredictability of Mediterranean agriculture, the precise qualities of what was being sold were not fixed at the time of the sale (*Ep.* 8.2; Morley 1996: 161–3; cf. Erdkamp 2005: 120–34). A far more extreme example of the impact of the environment on the distribution and availability of resources was the eruption of Vesuvius, devastating many of the famous Campanian vineyards and presenting producers in other regions with an opportunity to cash in, which seems to have induced some growers in southern Gaul to begin a significant expansion of their vineyards (Tchernia 1986: 221–53).

This, then, was the situation which Cicero imagined at Rhodes: the island was quite densely populated and a noted producer of wine, but not a major grain producer, so it was vulnerable to any poor harvest. Rhodes would not have been an obvious candidate for food crisis in earlier centuries, when its location and harbour facilities made it a major stopping-off point for traffic between Egypt and Athens (see [Dem.] 56; Pryor 1988: 54). However, its commercial position declined in the second century, and in 169 BCE it sent a request to the Roman Senate for a shipment of grain from Sicily (Polyb. 28.2.5). The technical limitations of ancient agriculture, together with the particular conditions of the environment, meant that every year many cities and regions were in this position, hoping for the arrival of grain merchants.

Far from being homogeneous, classical antiquity endured wide variations in the availability and quality of different goods, year on year. However, redistribution, let alone trade, was never the only available response, and it remains to consider the second part of the primitivist argument against the economic feasibility of widespread long-distance trade in the ancient world. Given the level of technological development, transport was slow and expensive: the question is whether it was so expensive that the movement of most goods was uneconomic unless subsidised or organised by the nobility or the state. Self-sufficiency was certainly a rational response to conditions of risk and uncertainty in agricultural production, but was it in fact the only available option for most people?

Ancient transport depended on the power of wind and muscle. Sailing could be quite fast and efficient if winds and currents were favourable, and otherwise slow and unreliable; rowing on the sea was expensive, given the numbers of men required to move any size of ship, so it was confined to military shipping; land transport was almost invariably slow, and the draught animals – oxen, mules, camels or humans – had to be fed. The main evidence for costs comes from Diocletian's Edict on Maximum Prices from 301 CE. The absolute figures for different sorts of transport are much less important than their relation to each other and to the prices of other goods; overall these suggest that transporting a load of grain a hundred miles overland would add over 50 per cent to its cost, while a hundred-mile journey over the sea would add only 2 per cent. The cost of river transport, according to a papyrus relating to the Nile, was a bit more than sea traffic (Duncan-Jones 1982: 368).

The implications of these calculations, however, can easily be exaggerated. Grain was particularly bulky and heavy relative to its value; freight charges would not raise the price of wine or oil to the same extent even if they were carried overland. The relative cheapness of sea travel is undeniable and fits with comparative evidence from later periods, but many parts of the ancient world were within reasonable reach of the sea or a navigable river. Moreover, the evidence from the Edict relates specifically to the maximum carriage charges that may be levied, not to the actual costs of transport – leaving aside the possibility that an imperial bureaucrat's view of an appropriate rate might not have wholly accorded with reality. The figures for sea travel relate to specific, well-travelled and, in the case of the Alexandria–Rome run, effectively subsidised routes, so are likely to be underestimates (Horden and Purcell 2000: 377). In any case a shipowner might calculate his costs quite differently, taking into account the invest-ment in his boat, the cost of upkeep and the likely risk; all the more so if he was also a merchant considering the potential for profit on a specific cargo, while perhaps subisidising his voyages by also transporting the goods of others. The cost of land transport is different if the merchant owns his own pack animals rather than hires those of others; he perhaps, but cer-tainly the farmer carrying his own goods to market, would think more in terms of time expended on the journey. Land transport might generally be slower than going by sea, but it could also be more reliable, with less risk of adverse weather conditions holding up the journey for weeks. What is clear is that the calculation of transport costs and the merits of different routes was more complicated than the Edict suggests, and there is no reason to suppose that costs were ever absolutely prohibitive.

The combination of environmental structures and the level of technol-ogy does not prevent movement, but it does shape and limit it. Sea and river transport did, in general, involve less 'friction', and the patterns of distri-bution of containers for goods like wine and oil often follow the coasts and navigable rivers. Ancient sources focused on the role of the Mediterranean, *mare nostrum*, in uniting different peoples and places; from Plato's image of the Greek cities 'like frogs around a pond', to the Elder Pliny's amazement, discussing the flax from which sails were made, that 'out of so small a seed springs the means of carrying the whole world to and fro' (*NH* 19.3–6), and a homily of John Chrysostom from the end of the fourth century CE: 'That we might easily keep up intercourse with distant countries, He spread the level of the sea between us, and gave us the swiftness of the winds, thereby making our voyages easier' (*Hom. in 1 Cor.* 34.7). This brings to mind the idea of the 'Middle Sea' as a space that can be crossed with relative ease and so brings different regions into contact with one another, hastening the spread of goods, taste and ideas: for example, the Baltic, the seas between China and Japan, the Sahara, and the Mediterranean (Abulafia 2005). It highlights the peculiar advantages of both Greece and Italy in having excep-tionally long coastlines, so that no part is too far from the sea; islands, too, far from being remote, are particularly accessible, so played a leading role in antiquity as sources of metals and other goods (Bresson 2005; Horden and Purcell 2000: 346). Such regions could better afford to become reliant on imported goods, since they had more frequent and reliable connections to the rest of the world. However, rivers could play a similar role, as seen for example in Strabo's account of the traffic along the River Baetis in Spain (3.2.3) or between the various rivers in southern Gaul (4.1.2, 4.1.14), or in the way that, when the Phoenicians closed off the traditional route for the supply of tin from Galicia via Gades (Cadiz), the Greeks developed an alternative route up the River Garonne in south-west France to the Bay of Biscay (Cunliffe 2001: 302–8).

The prevailing winds in the Mediterranean are from north-east to north-west; the prevailing current is anti-clockwise. This created favourable conditions on particular routes for long-distance travel, all other things being equal, but the majority of sea traffic hugged the coast, making use of local off-shore and on-shore breezes and currents around islands and headlands to travel in whichever directions they chose (Horden and Purcell 2000: 137–41). This was not necessarily successful; the long and troubled voyage of the apostle Paul and his captors from Caesarea to Rome included lengthy struggles against unfavourable winds, to the point where the sailors' efforts turned from trying to reach their destination to trying to reach a suitable harbour for over-wintering (Acts 27). The restricted sailing season described by writers from Hesiod in about 700 BCE to Vegetius in about 400 CE – 'From the third day before the ides of November until the sixth day before the ides of March, the seas are closed' (*Epitome Rei Militaris* 4.39) – was a matter of custom, and the calculation of risk versus profit, rather than a fixed rule: given sufficient inducement, such as might be offered by the authorities in a severe food crisis, shipowners might be persuaded to venture forth (Suet. *Claud.* 18–19). In some regions, the seas were not necessarily closed at all: 'Voyaging from Rhodes to Egypt is uninterrupted, and they could put the same money to work two or three times, whereas here they would have had to pass the winter and await the season for sailing' ([Dem.] 56.29).

Paul's voyage ended in disaster, as the ship was forced to run before a powerful northerly wind and then, having jettisoned much of its cargo and sailing gear, drifted in the Adriatic for a fortnight and was finally wrecked when the crew attempted to land on a beach. The Mediterranean is indeed prone to sudden and violent storms, and some of its coasts have fierce currents and dangerous rocks – Greek myth presented the perils of the Symplegades, the Clashing Rocks at the mouth of the Black Sea, and of Scylla and Charybdis, variously located between Sicily and Italy or off the coast of Africa (Synesius, *Ep.* 4.). Classical writers of all complexions regarded any kind of seafaring as highly dangerous, and sailing for the purposes of trade as nothing short of insanity:

Madness comes in different forms . . . A man may not be tearing his cloak and tunic, but he still needs a guardian if he fills his ship to the waterline with merchandise, putting only the width of a plank between himself and the sea, when his only reason for facing hardship and danger is silver cut into circles. (Juv. *Sat.* 14.284–91)

God did not make the sea for sailing on, but for the sake of the beauty of the element. The sea is tossed by storms; you ought to fear it, not to use it. The innocent element is not to blame; it is man's own rashness that puts him in peril. Someone who never goes to sea has no need to fear shipwreck. The sea is given to supply you with fish to eat, not for you to endanger yourself upon it; use it for food, not for commerce. (Ambrose, *De Elia* 70–1)

It is striking, of course, that such denunciations assume that a great many people are using the sea for precisely those purposes. Sailing was risky, even for the most skilful and experienced, to say nothing of the potential dangers from piracy or war. The high rates of interest attached to maritime loans – and the fact that taking interest at these rates was not considered extortionate – must reflect the likelihood of shipwreck as well as the potential profit of a successful voyage. They would not have been offered at all if there were not plenty of successful voyages.

Ancient ships and sailing techniques were adequate for the task; there was little development in either during the classical period, other than the construction of 'superfreighters' to carry exceptional cargoes like obelisks (Pliny, *NH* 16.201–2). Significant innovations were found, however, in handling cargo; above all, the production of amphorae for transporting liquids like wine and olive oil, in standard sizes, easily stacked and easily counted, and even, perhaps, becoming the 'brand' of a particular product, to judge from the way that some provincial amphorae are so similar to Italian containers in form that they may have been made in imitation of them (Peacock and Williams 1986: 93). The relative slowness of all forms of transport meant that most perishable goods were produced in the immediate vicinity of their market (see Morley 1996: 83–107 on the *suburbium* of Rome), but there were also technical solutions to the problem: drying fruit and meat, and above all preserving products such as olives, pork and fish in salt.

UNCERTAINTY

Because of their great passion for grain, merchants sail wherever they hear there is an abundance of it, across the Aegean, the Euxine and the Sicilian Sea, so that they can seize it. And when they have taken as much of it as they can onto their ships, they carry it across the sea, even storing it in the same ship in which they are sailing. And when they need money, they do not unload this grain anywhere they happen to be, but rather they take it and sell it wherever they hear that grain is selling for the highest price, where men place the highest value on it. (Xen. *Oec.* 20.27–8)

Where the speed of transport might become a serious problem was in mediating the availability and currency of information. Xenophon displays an assortment of typical aristocratic attitudes in his disparagement of merchants, but he accurately identifies their reliance on news of cheap supplies and high demand. In a world of periodic but unpredictable glut and dearth, this was one way of making a living. However, Xenophon seems to prefigure neoclassical economic theory in his lack of interest in the cost or accuracy of the information on which the merchants relied (cf. North 1981: 199). Juvenal's comment that 'wherever the hope of profit leads, a fleet will follow' (*Sat.* 14.79–80) is more to the point in its emphasis on hope, not certainty.

News in antiquity could travel no faster than a horse or a ship (Lee 1993; Lewis 1996). Some states invested heavily in improving their communications networks, to enhance military intelligence and ensure that the centre's orders were being obeyed. However, these networks did not reach everywhere, and the information they conveyed must rarely have been of economic import; occasionally, perhaps, news of a food crisis and a request for supplies. The most striking example comes from the fact that the date of a document was generally indicated by using the name of the reigning emperor – or at least the emperor whom the document's author believed to be reigning; in some of the more distant regions of Egypt, it could be weeks after the death of one emperor before the news arrived and the name of his successor started to be used (Duncan-Jones 1990: 7–8). Information that was of relevance primarily to traders was most probably conveyed by traders alone – and, as Cicero's example suggests, they might have reason to conceal their knowledge from competitors and customers alike.

When he found that trading in Bosporus was poor, as a war had broken out between Paerisades and the Scythian, and that there was no market for the merchandise which he had brought, he was in dire straits; for the creditors who had lent him money for the outward voyage were now demanding repayment. ([Dem.] 34.8)

Merchants operated in an environment of uncertainty, quite apart from the risks involved in travel; they needed to identify a potential bargain – even, by the Roman period, gambling on buying a share of the produce of a vineyard or olive grove well in advance of the harvest – and find a market for it within a reasonable period of time at a price that would cover their costs. A number of Athenian court cases from which speeches have survived involved traders either falling foul of the volatility of market prices or being accused of sharp practice in trying to get round that volatility (e.g. Dem. 32; [Dem.] 56; Lysias 22). One of the stories of archaic Greek trade, in which a ship was blown west rather than east, ended up in a previously unvisited part of Spain rather than in Egypt and 'consequently realised a greater return on their goods than any Greeks of whom we have precise knowledge, with the exception of Sostratus of Aegina' (Hdt. 4.152) could be considered part of the mythology of trade, embodying every merchant's dream. Even when the Mediterranean had been thoroughly explored, a capricious environment meant that such profits were still possible for the fortunate, and that a cargo of grain could probably find a market anywhere – but that certainly did not exclude the possibility of having to sell at a loss.

Various strategies were available. One was the common practice of carrying a mixed cargo, in the hope that something would always be saleable; the trading equivalent of self-sufficiency, reducing risk at the expense of missing out on the greatest profits. Even traders specialising in grain or wine were likely to carry pottery and other goods as well; it cannot be ruled out, for example, that the first Greek vases imported into Etruria were not the primary objects of trade at all, but simply ballast that turned out to be unexpectedly saleable (Gill 1991). Some goods were more reliable than others: less perishable, rarer, invariably in demand. A trader with sufficient access to resources to enter the trade in spices or incense would probably lose money only if the ship sank, even if the bulk of the profits went to the financiers.

Another approach was to cultivate a regular route, building up knowledge of the preferences of customers, perhaps establishing relationships with those customers and perhaps specialising in particular goods which would always find a market:

There was a Corinthian by the name of Demaratos, of the Bacchiad family, who chose to embark on a trading expedition and sailed to Italy in his own ship with his own cargo. He sold this cargo in the cities of Tyrrhenia [Etruria], which at that time were the most prosperous in the whole of Italy, and made a large profit. Thereafter he had no interest in visiting other ports but continued to sail the same route as before, carrying Greek cargo to the Tyrrhenians and Tyrrhenian cargo to Greece, and as a result he accumulated a large fortune. (Dion. Hal. 3.46)

In a similar way, some markets were more reliable than others: above all the great cities such as Athens, Alexandria, Rome and Constantinople, whose demand for the products of the world was almost insatiable. Trading activity gravitated towards such centres of consumption, and the major stops on the routes that led to them, because merchants could count on selling their cargoes at a profit.

Above all, merchants sought to acquire information. One of the most important developments over the course of classical antiquity was the expansion of knowledge of the world and the availability of advice on how to find one's way around it: information about routes, hazards, good harbours, and the specialised knowledge of the monsoon winds that allowed ships from the Mediterranean to trade directly with Arabia and India (Casson 1989; Nicolet 1991; Young 2001). Merchants might conceivably have consulted the encyclopaedic works of the geographers, but they also had their own handbooks: works like the *Expositio Totius Mundi*, which recorded, rather vaguely, the products of different regions and which peoples were said to be particularly sharp in their business practices, or the *Periplus Maris Erythraei*, noting what products were sold or in demand in different ports along the route to India, and giving advice on the likely attitudes of their rulers – 'obsessively acquisitive, always seeking to receive more, but in other respects a respectable person who speaks good Greek' (5).

More precise information, on current prices in different locations, was even more valuable, especially in the volatile grain market:

Some of these men would send off the goods from Egypt, others would travel on board with the shipments, and others would remain here in Athens and dispose of the merchandise. Then those who remained here would send letters to those abroad to inform them of the prevailing prices, so that if grain were expensive in Athens they might bring it here, and if the price should fall they might head to some other port. This was the main reason, men of the jury, why the price of grain rose: it was due to such letters and conspiracies. ([Dem.] 56.8)

When he arrived at Bosporus, carrying with him letters which I had written and given to him to deliver to my slave, who was over-wintering there, and also to a partner of mine – and in those letters I had stated the sum which I had lent to him, and the security, and asked them to inspect the goods as soon as they were unloaded and to keep an eye on them – the man simply did not deliver the letters which he had received from me, so that they might have no idea what he was doing. ([Dem.] 34.8)

Their [sc. the resident alien wholesalers'] interests are the opposite of other men's: they make the most profit when some bad news reaches the city and they can sell their grain for a high price. They are so delighted to hear of your disasters that they either get news of them before anyone else, or spread the rumours themselves. (Lysias 22.14)

All those involved in trade, merchants and financiers alike, sought to reduce their exposure to risk and improve their bargaining position by gathering information. They were, we may imagine, regularly thwarted, not only by their competitors' efforts (including, at least in Athens, the option of resorting to the law) but by time and distance. In an age of slow and fairly rudimentary communications, the ability of systems of distribution to remedy the effects of an unpredictable environment and the uneven distribution of resources was always limited. Even the city of Rome, the most reliable and insatiable market in the known world – 'so many merchant ships arrive here, conveying every kind of goods from every people every hour, every day, so that the city is like a marketplace common to the whole earth' (Aelius Aristides, *Or.* 27.11) – suffered from periodic panics about food shortages and rising prices. Smaller cities could only try to persuade merchants to visit regularly through the quality of their harbour or other facilities.

In such circumstances – certainly not because of the homogeneity of the environment – self-sufficiency and the avoidance of dependence on the market were an entirely rational, if rarely realisable, strategy. The peasant farmer might have realised greater profits by concentrating on crops for the market, or he might be forced to trade to be able to pay rents or taxes, but he might equally see his means of subsistence being shipped off to the consumers in the city because the price was better there. Even the market-orientated villas of Roman Italy, specialising in wine, oil or grain, aimed to supply most of their own subsistence needs rather than depend on the market. Urban consumers, of course, had no such choice. The market was unreliable, not – or not only – because of the profiteering of merchants, but because of the technological limitations of antiquity and the nature of its environment. This created an opportunity for systems of redistribution and for individuals to profit from them, but it also left trade in antiquity permanently associated with crisis, disaster and abrupt changes of fortune.

Thrasyllus the son of Pythodorus, of the deme Aescone, was once struck down by insanity as the result of luxurious living, so that he came to believe that all the ships putting into Peiraeus belonged to him, and he registered them as such in his accounts. He sent them off and carried out all the business for them, and when they returned from a voyage he received them with such exuberant happiness as if he was the sole owner of all the merchandise. Of course, if they were lost at sea he did not conduct any search for them, but if they came back safely he was openly delighted and spent his time feeling thoroughly satisfied. When his brother Crito arrived in Athens from Sicily, he was taken in charge and placed under the care of a doctor, who cured him of his insanity. But he often told the story of the way he had lived while he was mad, claiming that he had never in his whole life enjoyed himself more; for he was not affected by any distress, and on the other hand the sum of his pleasures was enormous. (Ath. *Deipnosophistae* 12.554e–f)

CHAPTER 3

Commodities and consumption

No one is allowed to import frankincense and similar foreign aromatics
to be used in religious rituals, or purple and other such dyes not native
to the country, or materials for any other purpose where imports from
abroad are inessential.

(Plato, *Laws* 847)

And the merchants of the earth shall weep and mourn over her; for no
man buyeth their merchandise any more: the merchandise of gold, and
silver, and precious stones, and of pearls, and fine linen, and purple,
and silk, and scarlet, and all thyine wood, and all manner vessels of
ivory, and all manner vessels of most precious wood, and of brass, and
iron . . . and fine flour, and wheat, and beasts, and sheep, and horses,
and chariots, and slaves, and souls of men.

(Revelation 18.11–13)

The limits of an exclusively ecological approach to the history of human
society are quickly reached when considering the nature of demand. As we
have already seen, the list of goods that might be considered essential in
a given situation, the limited availability and uneven allocation of which
might stimulate the development of systems of distribution, is long and
varied. It is certainly not determined by nutritional requirements alone;
except in famine situations, human diets reflect social and cultural preferences (Garnsey 1999). It can be useful to construct a model of the minimum
volume of grain required for the basic sustenance of a given population,
in order to estimate the carrying capacity of a region or to give an order
of magnitude for the minimum level of redistribution required to keep
people fed (Garnsey 1988; Hopkins 1983b). However, such models depend
on the deliberate exclusion of the social and ideological dimension: the
role of social and political structures in controlling and mediating access
to resources, and the role of subjective preferences in creating not just

'demand' but very specific sorts of demand, which are not always constant or predictable.

This is a particular problem in trying to explain developments over time. It is possible to construct more elaborate models of regional ecology which take into account the particular food preferences of a given population; thus we can estimate how far Roman Italy could meet the demands of its population for wine and olive oil as well as grain, or decide between different theories on the size of its population on the basis of the carrying capacity of the region (Morley 2001). Equally, the effects of changing population size or structure on the availability of resources and thus the role of demographic change as a stimulus to economic development can be modelled fairly easily (the problem for ancient history is invariably the shortage of evidence for population figures, agricultural yields, and so forth) on the assumption that demand will change in proportion to population size. The problem lies in explaining changes in the nature of demand itself, and yet these could have far-reaching consequences for social development, dramatically altering the picture of whether a given region should be seen as well or poorly endowed in resources relative to its population. Put crudely, the limited geographical distribution of tin becomes a problem only when a society develops a need for it despite the fact that it is not available locally – whereupon this becomes the stimulus for redirecting activity towards its acquisition. From an archaeological perspective – and only partly because of the nature of the evidence – key stages in social development are marked by significant changes in material practices; that is to say, changes in the nature and dimensions of demand, more often than not for exotic goods (e.g. C. Smith 1998). The study of the development of ancient trade has tended either to focus on the nature of demand at a given point in time or to treat change as something whose effects can be studied but whose causes remain a mystery. Neither approach seems wholly adequate.

CONSUMPTION

You say that you are poor, and I have to agree with you; anyone who is in need of a great many things is poor, and you are in need of a great many things because your desires are many and insatiable. (Basil of Caesarea, *In Divites* 56c–57b)

Economic theory tends to take demand for granted as the cause of scarcity; it focuses rather on the optimal allocation of resources to satisfy as far as possible the needs of individuals (Fine and Leopold 1993: 10). In so far as the demand for a particular good is analysed, it is assumed to be governed by price; as the price increases, at some point demand will decrease as potential purchasers either do without or substitute an alternative good. The nature or utility of the good is assumed to be adequately expressed by the extent to which it is 'substitutable'. Here, too, changes in the nature of demand are less easily modelled, as are many of the ways in which people actually behave in the market. The study of, in these terms, 'irrational' decision-making, such as the phenomenon whereby demand for a good falls if it is too cheap, because its quality is assumed to be inferior, belongs rather to sociology or social psychology: the study of consumption, or, in Foxhall's phrase, 'not demand but desire' (1998: 297).

'Demand is thus the economic expression of the political logic of consumption and thus its basis must be sought in that logic . . . Consumption is eminently social, relational, and active rather than private, atomic, or passive' (Appadurai 1986b: 31). It can serve as a form of display and competition for social status and power, and not only in the more spectacular (and economically incomprehensible) examples of conspicuous consumption or the 'conspicuous destruction' of *potlatch* rituals (Bocock 1993; Fine and Leopold 1993: 57; von Reden 1995a: 79–104). It can be a form of communication within society, establishing (perhaps quite unconsciously) one's social identity and adherence to communal values. It can, more often than not, be a site of argument and contestation, inextricably linked to other ideological structures. The problems of desire and of the need for desire to be limited and controlled were central to ancient moral and political debates; as Athenaeus said of Homer, 'he considered that passions and pleasures become very strong, and that foremost among them and innate are the desires for eating and drinking, and that they who abide resolutely in frugality are well-disciplined and self-controlled in all the exigencies of life' (*Deip.* 1.8e–9b). Examples of 'inappropriate' consumption – too much, too little, the wrong sort of thing in the wrong way at the wrong time with the wrong people – were offered in law courts and debating chambers as irrefutable evidence of the character flaws and suspect motives of political opponents (e.g. Edwards 1993; Davidson 1997).

The different meanings that accumulate around objects within a particular culture have implications for their use, including their potential for distribution. Some might be reserved for rulers; the way in which the sources of decorative marble, for example, were taken into imperial ownership under the Principate reflected a sense of what was appropriate as much as a practical decision to enhance imperial revenues, and in any case it established the basis of the distinctive structures of the extraction, distribution and sale of marble in the empire (Ward-Perkins 1971; Adam 2001).

The trade in purple dye extracted from the mollusc *murex* was also claimed as an imperial monopoly under the Principate for its association with the purple robes of the powerful (Reinhold 1970).

Much of the ancient debate on consumption was focused on food; indeed, Greeks and Romans have been described as 'obsessed' with this subject (Garnsey 1999: xi). This was not confined to foodstuffs that were unusual, whether because of their cost, their rarity, their exotic origin or their association with barbarians or foreigners; the most basic elements of the diet acquired a range of cultural associations which both reflected and influenced how they were consumed. Wine, for example, was a marker of civilisation, but only if consumed in moderate quantities and mixed with water rather than neat; it was both an essential component of various kinds of social gathering and a potential source of disruption and unrest; and, as we have seen, an enormous range of different varieties and qualities of wine made it possible (indeed, unavoidable) to convey subtle messages about social standing, adherence to the conventions of friendship and hospitality and so forth (Purcell 1985; Tchernia 1986; Murray 1990; Garnsey 1999: 128–38). The wine trade both responded to and helped to realise the desire for social differentiation.

The symbolic weight attached to bread as the staple foodstuff of antiquity is unsurprising, but we might take a step back and consider the basis for the choice between bread and porridge as different ways of consuming grain (Garnsey 1999: 15, 120–2). Nutritionally there may be little to choose between them. Grain in the form of bread is portable and easier to eat 'on the go', but becomes inedible more quickly; bread can be refined significantly, thus offering a greater possibility of differentiation between types, even if that included adulteration with chalk to improve its whiteness (Pliny, *NH* 8.114; Ath. *Deip.* 3.108–15), whereas porridge remained simply porridge, an irredeemably vulgar food; bread required far more preparation and elaborate equipment for processing the grain. Whatever the reasons, this choice was inexplicable in purely economic or ecological terms, but was both economically and ecologically significant. In the first place, porridge provides liquid as well as sustenance while the consumer of bread requires an accompanying drink; the move from *puls* to *panis* in late Republican Italy has consequently been suggested as the reason for the contemporaneous expansion of viticulture (Tchernia 1982; Purcell 1985). Secondly, not all grains make good bread; the taste for this product inspired the gradual replacement of barley with wheat as the main crop of many areas of the Mediterranean, despite wheat's greater susceptibility to drought and thus an increased possibility of food crisis, and the move from hulled wheat to different varieties of naked wheat (Sallares 1991: 313–72). Since the wheat that made the best bread was less suited to the Mediterranean climate, the demand for higher-quality products often had to be met through some form of distribution of grain from wetter regions such as Gaul or the northern Balkans. Further, not every region had local supplies of rock suitable for millstones (Peacock 1980).

LUXURIES AND STAPLES

Arabia is styled 'Fortunate' – a country with a false and misleading name, for it suggests that her happiness is due to the favour of the powers above, whereas she owes more of it to the powers of darkness. Arabia's fortune derives from the fact that mankind is luxurious even when it comes to death, when they burn over the deceased the products which were originally understood to be created for the gods. It is declared on good authority that Arabia does not produce in a year so large a quantity of perfume as was burned by the emperor Nero in a day at the funeral of his wife Poppaea. Then calculate the vast number of funerals celebrated every year throughout the entire world, and the perfumes – those that are given to the gods a single grain at a time – that are piled up in heaps to the honour of dead bodies . . . At a minimum, India, China and the Arabian peninsula take from our empire 100 million sesterces every year – that is what our luxuries and our women cost us. (Pliny, *NH* 12.83–4)

It is conventional, in the study of the objects of ancient trade, to distinguish between 'luxuries' on the one hand and 'staples' or 'necessities' on the other, and to assume that only the latter were of any significance. The primitivist argument about environmental homogeneity and transport costs discussed in the last chapter was aimed entirely at refuting the idea that there could have been an extensive trade in staple goods in antiquity; it is freely admitted that exotic goods of high value relative to their weight and bulk were always traded, but the market for such items is assumed to be small, so the volume and value of traffic must have been insufficient to support many traders. 'The trade with Arabia Felix, India and China has excited more interest among both ancient writers and modern historians owing to the exotic character of the goods which it handled, the high prices paid for them, and the romantic lands which it penetrated. Its volume, however, must have been small, since it catered for a minute, very wealthy minority' (Jones 1974: 149–50). Interestingly, modernising historians share the view that luxuries are synonymous with superfluity and economic insignificance; their disagreement with the primitivist perspective is about the level and regularity of trade in staple goods.

At first sight this is an entirely reasonable and natural distinction, and it certainly represents a valid criticism of the habit of automatically ascribing great significance to any movement of any sort of goods in antiquity. However, on closer inspection these categories appear less straightforward and natural, embodying some problematic assumptions. How, for example, is a luxury actually to be defined? The term tends to conflate intrinsic qualities of the object in question, such as its origin, its portability and the fact that it is clearly unnecessary for sustenance, with its value in the marketplace and the identity of its ultimate consumers. Put another way, we generally know a luxury when we see one, without being able to explain exactly why, and without any assurance that our view would be universally shared; in modern western society, a car might be, but is not necessarily, considered a luxury. The concept of 'necessity', once the absolute minimum needs of subsistence have been met, is equally elusive and contestable. In classical antiquity, fine wheat bread might be a luxury as much as a necessity, and wine a necessity – as a source of liquid free from the risk of infection – as much as a luxury; the simple dichotomy is inadequate to convey the place of such objects in ancient economy and society. Rostovtzeff in fact stumbled across the problem in trying to characterise goods that seemed to him to fall between the two categories:

The growing prosperity of the cities of the Empire increased the demand for articles of finer quality, which were not exclusively luxuries but mostly things ministering to the comfort of civilized men, such as the better brands of coloured woollen and linen stuffs and of leather ware, more or less artistic furniture, fine silver plate, perfumes and paints, artistic toilet articles, spices and the like. These things became more and more necessities of life for the city population throughout the empire. (1957: 169)

This recognition of the cultural relativity of needs and desires echoes the arguments of eighteenth-century political economists against the use of the term 'luxury' in economic analysis:

By necessaries I understand, not only the commodities which are indispensably necessary for the support of life, but whatever the custom of the country renders it indecent for creditable people, even of the lowest order, to be without. A linen shirt, for example, is strictly speaking not a necessity of life. The Greeks and the Romans lived, I suppose, very comfortably though they had no linen. But in the present times, through the greater part of Europe, a creditable day-labourer would be ashamed to appear in public without a linen shirt, the want of which would be supposed to denote that disgraceful degree of poverty which, it is presumed, nobody can well fall into without extreme bad conduct. (A. Smith 1976 [1776]: v.ii.k.3)

Adam Smith was arguing against the long-standing tendency to interpret the growth of trade and a general increase of material prosperity in terms of the classical condemnations of 'luxury' (Sekora 1977; Berry 1994; Winch 1996). There is no ignoring the importance of this term for Greek and especially Roman political discourse, where it served both as an all-purpose accusation against any opponent and as a persuasive explanation of social disorder and decline (Edwards 1993). Seventeenth- and eighteenth-century commentators, often employing classical pseudonyms like 'Britannicus', projected the anxieties of these ancient sources about the debilitating and feminising effects of conspicuous consumption onto their own society and argued on this basis for legislation to regulate the consumption of various goods (Morley 1998).

The response of political economists such as Smith was to highlight the vapidity of the idea of 'luxury', redefining it as 'refinement' and emphasising the fluid, subjective nature of desire and demand. More importantly, they argued that new patterns of consumption should be seen as an index of national prosperity and strength; the paradox of luxury was that, in a phrase originally coined by Bernard Mandeville in his *Fable of the Bees* in 1732, 'private vice' gave rise to 'public benefit'.

In the present imperfect state of society, luxury, though it may proceed from vice or folly, seems to be the only means that can correct the unequal distribution of property. The diligent mechanic, and the skilful artist, who have obtained no share in the division of the earth, receive a voluntary tax from the possessors of land; and the latter are prompted, by a sense of interest, to improve those estates, with whose produce they may purchase additional pleasures. (Gibbon 1994 [1776]: 80)

Economists have long since abandoned the term 'luxury'; they might refer instead to goods with high-income elasticity of demand – that is, things one buys only when feeling particularly prosperous – but in other respects these are indistinguishable from other goods. Ancient historians, however, have retained not only the term but, without always realising it, much of its moralising baggage. This is unhelpful in two respects. In the first place, as already noted, the term 'luxury' conflates several different attributes of objects and their economic implications. The value of an item relative to its bulk and thus to the cost of transporting it to market is certainly important in determining the parameters of its distribution; so too the level of demand for it. Exotic origin and apparent superfluity are already accounted for in the calculation of transport costs and the level of demand; there are no grounds, therefore, for distinguishing in material terms between different *categories* of object of trade, let alone for assuming that objects in one category are *per se* economically trivial and redundant.

The history of trade in late medieval and early modern Europe highlights the implausibility of such an assumption. Grain began to be traded on a large scale relatively late, and only between specific locations under special circumstances; the total volume being traded in the seventeenth-century Mediterranean was less than one per cent of the amount consumed (Braudel 1982: 403, 456–7). The major items of distribution were scarcely 'staples': high-quality wool, distinctive textiles, pottery, fish, and goods from the East and the Americas such as pepper, tea, coffee, chocolate and sugar (Braudel 1981: 220–7; Tracy 1990; Chaudhury and Morineau 1999). The main driver of trade was not necessity but the development of new patterns of consumption. 'Luxury goods' were not solely the prerogative of the rich; many of them, such as pepper (to make salted meat palatable) or tea (to make boiled water palatable) were used in very small quantities, but the aggregate demand was nevertheless considerable.

The ancient evidence needs to be considered in this light. The 'Muziris papyrus' from Egypt, which records on one side the terms of a loan taken out to finance a voyage from India and on the other a list of goods (presumably the cargo from that voyage), their values and the duties levied on them, gives some indication of the amount of money and potential profits involved in ancient trade with the East (*P.Vinob.* G 40822 = Rupprecht 1993: 61–4; Casson 1990; Young 2001: 47–69; Rathbone 2003). This activity was certainly not economically trivial, even if it did serve only a small number of customers. As for the commerce in 'staples', the grain trade, outside the supply of a few permanent consumers such as Athens and Rome, was far more dependent on harvest and market fluctuations than trade in wine or spices, with greater potential for both profits and disaster; the simple fact that it involved a basic foodstuff does not automatically make it more significant in terms of the overall volume of activity. The trade in slaves in antiquity was undoubtedly substantial, with tens of thousands of human beings being trafficked every year; this merchandise, at least in part, was destined for 'unproductive' uses, ministering to the desires and enhancing the status of those who purchased it (Bradley 1994: 32–8; Scheidel 1997; Cartledge 2001).

A second objection to the conventional condemnation of 'luxury goods' is that it tends to value objects purely in economic terms. Trade in incense, for example, might not have involved many individuals or contributed significantly to antiquity's gross domestic product compared with the vast volume of agricultural production, but it delivered an item that was essential for the worship of the gods on whose favour the harvest depended. Slaves may or may not have played a significant role in production, but classical society was inconceivable without them. In many cases, the qualities of goods that truly mattered were not their economic value but their role in social interaction or differentiation and in the legitimation and maintenance of political structures. Distribution was, one might say, driven by the need to obtain the things without which society would not properly function (Foxhall 1998: 298). This has to be understood in terms of specific patterns of consumption and desire, not in terms of a fixed demand for 'necessities'.

This approach also offers a more productive way of thinking about the concept of 'luxury', a term which is eminently dispensable for a strictly materialist economic history but vital for understanding Greek and Roman conceptions, which in turn influenced their behaviour. Luxury is best understood not as an intrinsic quality of particular objects but as a form of consumption; some objects might be better suited or more commonly associated with it, but potentially any good – even bread or wine – could be consumed luxuriously (Appadurai 1986b: 38). Within ancient discourse, in contrast to modern attitudes, *luxuria* or *truphē* were automatically condemned; the question was whether a particular piece of behaviour was considered – or, given that this debate was frequently conducted in law-courts or assemblies, could be presented as – appropriate or excessive, socially acceptable or potentially disruptive. Part of the meaning of ancient trade was that, in the eyes of commentators such as the Elder Pliny, it was associated with and contributing towards excessive, luxurious consumption. One might speculate whether, as in the eighteenth century, this moral anxiety was actually a reflection of growing, and more widely dispersed, material prosperity and the development of new (but potentially disruptive) economic structures.

Certainly it should not be assumed that the ancient condemnation of luxury and the idealisation of frugality would have served as an impediment to the development of widespread distribution of goods. Other facets of the elite code of behaviour placed equal weight on the importance of lavish consumption, in generosity to one's friends and dependants, service to the city and living a lifestyle appropriate to one's station. These, clearly, created desires and demands.

THE CAPACITY TO CONSUME

The main contribution of the debate about luxuries and staples has been to draw attention to the question of the capacity of different groups within

ancient society to consume. The key to this question is the level of agricultural surplus, something for which, unfortunately, we have almost no
direct evidence (Garnsey 1999: 22–9). It is clear enough that, from the eighth
century if not before, Greek society was producing a sufficiently large and
reliable surplus to support social differentiation in burials and other material practices – expressed above all in the consumption of imported goods
by the elite (Morris 1987; Tandy 1997: 19–58). Near Eastern societies had
developed elaborate social structures before this date; Italy, Gaul and Spain
showed such symptoms a little later, partly under the influence of contact
with Phoenicians and Greeks (Cunliffe 2001). The total amount of wealth
later disposed of by classical Athens, the Hellenistic kingdoms and the
Roman Empire was clearly considerable; the evidence suggests significant
increases in population alongside extensive building works, both public
and private, and the expansion of both military and cultural activity. Compared with the expansion of global wealth and productivity over the last two
centuries this development was more or less negligible, but some periods
of ancient history can compare favourably with any other pre-industrial
society (Millett 2001; Saller 2002).

Throughout classical antiquity wealth was divided unevenly between
the community and the individuals and families within it, and between
different individuals and households. The resources at the disposal of the
community as a whole (especially as this developed into 'the state') were
immensely important in shaping patterns of consumption and distribution;
this will be considered below. The existence of wealthy elites in every region,
even in egalitarian societies such as classical Athens, is again not in doubt,
and their preferences and practices of consumption were certainly significant in creating the conditions for widespread distribution of many different
goods, even if not in vast quantities. The real question is about the level of
'mass consumption'; whether ancient society was simply divided between a
'mass' living barely above subsistence level and the elite who appropriated
much of their surplus production and also drew on the labour of slaves, or
whether economic and social differences were more finely graded (cf. de
Ste Croix 1981; Wood 1988; Atkins and Osborne forthcoming).

The fact that many classical societies divided up their citizen populations according to gradations of wealth strongly suggests the existence of
a range of groups, even if it is not possible to determine how many –
how great a majority – belonged to the relatively impoverished *thētes* or
proletarii; so does the practice of members of citizen militias having to be
able to afford to provide their own weapons. To touch for a moment on
another long-running historical debate, it seems entirely implausible that all

Athenian farmers owned slaves, but the fact that some certainly did – and not only the very rich – is another indication of differing levels of prosperity in Attic society (Jameson 1977; Wood 1988; Cartledge 2001). Similarly, not all Italian peasants could afford to own oxen, but those who could would then have enjoyed a significant advantage in agricultural productivity and surplus production (Jongman 1988). Evidence on the size of land-holdings in different regions implies the existence of farmers of 'middling' prosperity, while it has recently been argued that a majority of Egyptians in the Roman period could be described as 'sleek', enjoying a level of material prosperity well above subsistence level (Garnsey and Saller 1987: 66–71; Rathbone forthcoming). It is clear that the disposal of a significant surplus and hence the capacity to consume was not confined to a tiny elite, even if the circumstances of many will have varied significantly from year to year and from generation to generation; the rich, one might suggest, were those who could generally count on maintaining their choice of lifestyle regardless of the success of the harvest.

Even the poor peasant farmers who formed the majority of the population in all periods of antiquity had to produce some level of surplus in order to pay taxes and rents; they would also aim to be able to store at least a year's supplies (Garnsey 1999: 25–8). In bad years they might go hungry or fall into debt, but a good harvest could leave them with resources to spare. Evidence for peasant lifestyles comes predominantly from elite literary sources; it varies between hopeless optimism and a tendency to exaggerate the simplicity and anti-materialism of rustic life – often in the same text. Farmers were never wholly isolated from society or wholly divorced from the market; depending on local resources, many would have needed to buy goods such as salt, olive oil, shoes, clothing, pottery and tools (Frayn 1979; Evans 1980; de Ligt 1990). The Roman agronomist Cato was not actually a poor peasant, but his handbook does give an impression of the range of goods which a farmer might *like* to have at his disposal: 'Tunics, togas, blankets, smocks and shoes should be bought at Rome; caps, iron tools, scythes, spades, mattocks, axes, hammers, ornaments and small chains at Cales and Minturnae; spades at Venafrum; carts and sledges at Suessa and in Lucania; jars and pots at Alba and at Rome; tiles from Venafrum' (*De Agricultura* 135). These were not regular purchases; tools would be expected to last, and in a bad year shoes and clothing might have to be patched rather than replaced. A good year, however, offered an opportunity: to renew worn-out items, add to the farm's equipment, enjoy an improved diet, pay for a suitably lavish wedding or funeral. A very bad year or an accident or illness, threatening the survival of the household, might be the stimulus to a different form of consumption; rural shrines in Italy in the fourth and third centuries BCE contain thousands of cheap terracotta votives, many in the shape of limbs or other body parts, offered in the hope of or in thanks for divine favour (Steingräber 1980). None of these demands amounted to very much on an individual or household basis, but the aggregate demand of millions of peasants – some of whom may sometimes also have been able to participate in the more elaborate forms of consumption discussed below – was potentially enormous.

PLEASURE, DISCRIMINATION AND FASHION

Within the city of Rome, no one is allowed to wear trousers or boots . . . We command that no one shall be permitted to wear very long hair, and no one, not even a slave, shall wear garments made of skins. (*Codex Theodosianus* 14.10.3, 4)

Other members of ancient society were in a position to participate more fully in social life and to lead a more comfortable, varied and materially elaborate existence. Their patterns of consumption can be considered in terms of different registers: utility, pleasure, solidarity, differentiation, politics; in practice, of course, they were always multi-dimensional. An increased consumption of meat had its utilitarian aspect in so far as it improved the nutritional quality of the diet; it served the interests of pleasure in both flavour and texture; it was associated with the communal rituals of the civic sacrifice, while the ability to consume it more regularly undoubtedly worked as a means of differentiating oneself from the predominantly vegetarian masses – something which might then be regarded with suspicion in the context of the egalitarian *polis*, or through the association of excessive meat-eating with barbaric northerners (Garnsey 1999: 65–8).

Clothing is a necessity; clothes made from high-quality wool or silk also offer pleasure and comfort. The clearest evidence for the importance of pleasure in shaping consumption patterns comes from food. Salt, for example, is a nutritional requirement in only very small doses, but it was essential to bring out flavours: 'a civilised life is impossible without salt' (Pliny, *NH* 31.88; Forbes 1955: 157–74). The wish to introduce some degree of pleasure into the unending and monotonous consumption of cereals prompted a move from porridge to bread and placed great emphasis on the importance of accompaniments – *opson* in Greek – and flavourings such as pepper and fish sauce (*garum*), expensive but strongly flavoured, so they were used in minute quantities (cf. Pliny, *NH* 13.93–4 and Curtis 1991). 'The fact that one set of herbs is dedicated to seasoning shows that it used to be customary to gather all one's ingredients at home, and that there was no demand for Indian pepper and the other luxuries that we import from overseas' (*NH* 19.58). Pliny's use of the past tense clearly implies that the use of such spices was now commonplace; our evidence for their use relates to elaborate elite cuisine, not the diet of the masses, but comparative evidence suggests that the consumption of such goods is not necessarily confined to the very wealthy (Hobhouse 1985; Braudel 1981: 220–7). It is precisely those whose diet is basic and unvaried who will have the greatest need for flavourings.

Patterns of consumption always have an important social dimension. Consciously or not, people follow the customs of their society in food, dress and other material practices and thereby reaffirm their membership and identity; Greeks ate a particular diet and thought of it as peculiarly Greek. Put another way, society established norms, which created a need for certain goods. There were accepted modes of dress, for example; not only for everyday wear (including, for Athenian women, the need for *peplos* brooches: Foxhall 1998) but different clothing for religious rites and other special occasions – white, more expensive to produce and needing to be cleaned more often (Kleijwegt 2002). There were established norms for consumption in the context of religious ritual (incense, spices, burnt offerings, clothing), weddings (spices, special fruits, clothing) and funerals (incense, the deliberate destruction of property – compare Plut. *Sol.* 20.5, 21.5 on the need to limit the volume of textiles thus sacrificed – and the construction of a suitable monument) (Detienne 1977; Morris 1992: 103–55). Gatherings for the purpose of consumption, of wine or food, were vital forces for social cohesion – the great civic sacrifices and festivals, bringing citizens together – and for reinforcing the solidarity of smaller groups, in aristocratic drinking parties and in the dinners held by groups of officials and members of voluntary organisations (Murray 1990; Slater 1991; Garnsey 1999: 128–33).

Most of these forms of consumption, and many others, could also be used as means of social differentiation. This aspect is rather more prominent in our sources than normal, taken-for-granted practices, since it was frequently regarded as morally and politically problematic. In a self-consciously egalitarian society such as democratic Athens, deviation from norms of consumption could always be interpreted as an attack on the values of the *polis*: the purchase of fresh sea-perch seemed undemocratic to the seller or consumer of small fry (Ar. *Wasps* 493–5), while the accusation of *opsophagia*, eating relishes as if they were a basic foodstuff, was a serious accusation to make against a political opponent (Xen. *Mem.* 3.14; generally Davidson 1997). The archaeology of Athenian houses suggests that they were broadly similar until the second half of the fourth century, when large and lavishly decorated ones begin to be built (Nevett 1999; Dem. *Olyn.* 25–6). Athens succeeded to some extent in limiting social differentiation in material practices during this period, but the need to police practices such as the *symposium*, the upper-class drinking party, makes it clear that 'excessive' consumption continued nevertheless (Schmitt-Pantel 1990).

In other societies differentiation was embedded in the social structure, creating demands for goods with which to establish superior social status. The Spartan communal meal ended with competition between the wealthiest elders in the provision of desserts (Fisher 1989). The Hellenistic monarchies established the model, later followed by the Romans, for expressing and establishing the ruler's superior power and status through lavish and distinctive uses of precious metals, spices, elaborate clothing, and so forth. The Roman elite marked themselves out through dress, diet, housing, drinking practices, dinner parties, slaves and citrus-wood tables; further, they developed elaborate but unwritten rules about the correct ways of consuming such objects, to distinguish the true aristocrat from someone who could merely afford to live like one (Veyne 1961; Edwards 1993). However, the degree of activity at this level of society does not mean that there was no attempt at social differentiation among the lower orders, nor that there was a complete separation between elite and popular consumption.

One of the founding theorists of the study of consumption suggested the opposite: taste diffuses slowly through society through imitation (Veblen 1970 [1899]). The elite always have a need for novelty and exoticism, using prestige items to differentiate themselves from the mass and to compete amongst themselves; a new form of consumption, if it proves successful, is first imitated by other members of the elite and then by those lower down in society, so that the elite must again strive to differentiate themselves. The change from porridge to bread must first have occurred in elite households, as it presupposes facilities for milling and baking. The masses followed, with the establishment of commercial bakeries, so that barley, the previous staple, comes to be seen initially as food for the poor and then as fit only for animal fodder. The elite, meanwhile, began to insist on finer-quality wheat flour. The same process can be seen in wine and clothing, as the range of options expands to accommodate differentiation not only between but within the broad categories of 'affordable' and 'expensive'.

A further function of consumption may be to establish or perform a specific social role. Some Roman freedmen may have imitated the fictional Trimalchio in trying to imitate elite practices; others pursued a distinctive strategy of epigraphic commemoration, both to emphasise their status as citizens and, in some cases, to advertise their professions, implicitly rejecting aristocratic disparagement of trade and manufacturing (Joshel 1992). Another example is the use of cosmetics and perfume, as women sought to mark themselves off from one another in the competition for men (compare Xenophon's character Ischomachus on the subject of his wife's make-up: 'These tricks might perhaps succeed in deceiving a stranger, but people who spend their whole lives together will certainly be discovered if they try to deceive one another'; *Oec.* 10.8) (Forbes 1955: 24–49). These were certainly considered problematic by male commentators – 'the most superfluous of all forms of luxury, for pearls and jewels can be inherited by the heir of their wearer, and clothes last for some time, but perfumes lose their scent at once' (Pliny, *NH* 13.20) – but that did not make them dispensable.

Imitation of the social elite was not the only way in which patterns of consumption might change; there was also the imitation of other cultures, especially in the aftermath of conquest. 'Persian' practices appeared in Athens in the aftermath of the successful defence of Greece (Miller 1997). The process can be seen most clearly in the western provinces of the Roman Empire; rather than a top-down process of officially imposed 'Romanisation', archaeologists now see a deliberate choice by native populations to express a Roman identity through patterns of dress, diet and housing. This created a demand for 'Roman' goods – wine, olive oil, *terra sigillata*, roof tiles – that had to be met through new production techniques and imports (Woolf 1997: 1–23, 169–205). By the end of the fourth century, however, the growing power of a new group with its own distinctive patterns of consumption inspired imitation, forcing the emperors to intervene to forbid the wearing of such barbarous garb as trousers. The wearing of trousers and boots could perhaps have been prompted by their convenience and utility, but the wearing of long hair in the barbarian style can only be described as fashion.

CITIES AND WARS

The greatest resources in antiquity were disposed of by 'public' institutions, above all the state; activities carried on at a communal or social level were always more important in creating a demand for goods than any patterns of private consumption. This section will focus on two important activities: urbanisation and warfare.

The ancient world was distinguished by its cities; they were regarded as essential for civilised life (even if the majority of the population lived outside them and visited only for markets and festivals), and almost every period of classical antiquity saw a significant increase in their number and in the size of the total urban population. It is impossible to establish plausible population figures for more than a few exceptional cities, but for the Roman Empire it has been estimated that about eight or nine million people in a total population of about 50–60 million were town dwellers: Rome by the time of Augustus contained a million of them, Constantinople and Alexandria at their respective heights contained perhaps half a million each. In earlier periods the figures are less spectacular but still impressive.

Urbanisation developed above all as a result of the decision to invest a significant portion of society's surplus production in centralisation and the built environment. The city was a means of establishing and reinforcing political, ideological and economic power (Mann 1986: 1–28). In some cases this was the power of an elite; the city became their arena for competition for prestige, influence and office that served at the same time to reinforce their collective dominance over the rest of society (e.g. Patterson 1991; Woolf 1997: 124–6). In other instances it was the power of a single ruler, setting himself apart from potential rivals and competing with his predecessors; in others, seen most spectacularly in Athens' commemoration of itself in the Parthenon, the power of the *polis* itself against other states (Castriota 1992).

Power was expressed and established through grandiose building projects – temples, assembly halls, theatres, gymnasia, bath houses and aqueducts – which required huge quantities of bricks, tiles, stone, marble and all kinds of wood (see Meiggs 1982). Social cohesion was promoted through festivals and games, which equally involved lavish expenditure. The lifestyles of the landed elite who made the cities their main residence and place of display needed to be supplied with the requisite goods. All of these activities gave employment to craftsmen and other workers, whose needs also had to be supplied: urbanisation creates consumers, in the sense of people who rely on others to produce their food and on systems of distribution. The role of cities in the magnification of power meant that the grain supply often had to be underwritten by the ruler or rulers, to keep the peace, and in the case of Rome and Constantinople elaborate systems for the mobilisation and distribution of grain collected as tax were developed (Garnsey 1988; Herz 1988; Veyne 1990; Sirks 1991). Even this, however, depended on the involvement of private shipowners to transport the *annona*, while the demands of urban populations for other goods (with the exception of the great Roman imperial capitals, which at some points in their history also received state distributions of wine, oil and pork) could be met only through private systems of distribution; the generosity of the elite might supply a few, but most relied on the market. The profits to be made in supplying the demands of the great capitals in turn supported the growth of other cities as ports and centres where goods could be collected together for onwards shipment, whose populations then added their own requirements to the total volume of demand (Morley 1996: 176–7; Young 2001 on Palmyra and Alexandria).

The common characterisation of the ancient city as a 'consumer city' is based, once again, on a potentially misleading contrast with an idealised version of the late medieval 'producer city' (Weber 1958; Finley 1981b; Morley 1996: 14–20). The ancient city was indeed both a place for consumption and, so to speak, a form of consumption. Far from acting as an impediment to trade and economic development, however, it was precisely this that gave the phenomenon of urbanisation its economic significance. The growth of cities in antiquity created a demand that could for the most part be met only through trade. Even where the city was small enough to subsist normally from its hinterland, resources (time, if not money) had to be invested in moving the surplus from the country to the urban centre; this created conditions in which professional middlemen might take over some of the tasks of transporting and retailing goods. When the harvest was poor, peasants could turn to hunting or scavenging, but town-dwellers could only hope for the arrival of merchants or the intervention of the political elite to bring in supplies (Garnsey 1988; Hopkins 1983b).

Warfare was likewise a defining characteristic of classical culture (Vernant 1968; Garlan 1975); it might in some cases be a form of acquisition – the profitability of imperialism is equally clear in the Athenian and the Roman cases – but it was undoubtedly a form of consumption, and thus created further demands for goods. In Athens and Republican Rome, part of the cost was passed on to individual citizens of sufficient wealth, but the state still paid for their maintenance – and the fact that in Athens this was provided in cash implies the involvement of private traders in supplying food to the army. Many classical and Hellenistic states employed mercenaries on a cash basis; Rome employed a combination of cash payments and the redistribution of goods collected as tax, such as grain and oil – but even here, the absence of any 'merchant navy' makes it clear that the state presupposed the existence and co-operation of a substantial volume of private commercial transport. Ever-lengthening military campaigns, together with the stationing of significant numbers of troops in the sparsely settled margins of the empire, towards the limits of cereal production, where they could obtain at best only part of their basic requirements locally, created ever greater demands on systems of distribution (Whittaker 1983: 118; 1994: 60–97, 99–104). Over time, local production might develop sufficiently to provide a greater proportion of the army's needs, but in some regions they would always have to rely on supplies from outside – and all the more so for goods such as oil, *garum*, leather and metals. The army of northern Britain, it has been calculated, needed twelve thousand calves per annum simply to repair and replace its tents, while a single legionary fortress has yielded 20 tons of iron nails (Breeze 1984; Pitts 1985; Drummond and Nelson 1994: 80).

The army undoubtedly played a role in the diffusion of tastes to the regions in which it was stationed – the same can be said for Greek soldiers in Asia during the Hellenistic period – and in the education of recruits from less civilised regions in the 'proper' forms of consumption. The proceeds of the conquests of Alexander and the generals of Rome both fuelled consumption in their capitals and imported new customs and desires. Above all, simply by taking citizens away from their farms for a while and sending them into less hospitable territory, warfare created a need for the distribution of the most basic items of existence.

COMMODITIES

No good is intrinsically a commodity – that is to say, an object whose primary purpose is market exchange. Rather, commoditisation is a phase in the 'social life' of an object, 'the situation in which its exchangeability (past, present, or future) for some other thing is its socially relevant feature' (Appadurai 1986b: 13), and not necessarily of all objects. Many goods in antiquity were exchanged as gifts or redistributed by the state or by powerful individuals; many were consumed by their producers. However, the evidence suggests that market exchange became increasingly important in the course of classical antiquity, and most goods had the *potential* to be commoditised.

This could create social and ideological problems. All societies, even in the modern, market-dominated West, seek to set limits on what kinds of items should be distributed solely according to the ability to pay; consider current debates about access to healthcare and education, or the modern abhorrence of slavery and the anxiety surrounding situations, such as prostitution, where human beings may appear to be treated as commodities (see Kopytoff 1986). Certain items in antiquity were removed from exchange altogether and reserved for rulers or the state; in many regions of Greece in the archaic period, land was inalienable, at least in theory, in an attempt to ensure the stability and continuity of the community (Morris 1986; cf. Tandy 1997: 112–38). Other goods were available for commoditisation, but not without debate. The ancients had no objection to the sale of human beings in general, but the enslavement of Greeks was clearly problematic; working for a wage or a fee came to be seen as a form of 'self-enslavement' (Xen. *Mem.* 1.2), making oneself into a commodity. The sense that there was something profoundly wrong in basic foodstuffs becoming wholly subject to the market permeated not only the regulation of grain supplies, as in Lysias' condemnation of non-citizen grain traders as the enemies of the state, but discussions of other goods:

In Rome, a garden was once a poor man's farm; the plebs got their market supplies from a garden . . . By Hercules, how little this produce costs and how adequate it is both for pleasure and for filling you up, and yet here we meet the same disgraceful situation as everywhere else. Perhaps it would be tolerable for some fruits to be grown which, because of their flavour or size or portentous shape, are not for the poor . . . But have distinctions been discovered even in herbs? Has wealth now established grades even in articles of food that sell for a single bronze coin? The poor declare that even among vegetables there are now some kinds being grown that are not for them . . . It would surprise us if cattle were not allowed to feed on thistles, but they are forbidden to the poor! (Pliny, *NH* 19.52–4)

The view of commoditisation as a threat to social order offers one way of thinking about Aristotle's well-known distinction between household management (*oikonomia*) and money-getting (*chrēmatistikē*) (von Reden 1995a; Meikle 1995). Both involved the sale of goods for money in order to purchase other goods. However, in household management the commodity phase of the objects involved is intended to last as briefly as possible; surplus goods are sold expressly in order to purchase commodities that the household lacks, which are immediately converted into objects of consumption for socially desirable ends. In *chrēmatistikē*, however, the objects remain commodities for far longer: the merchant buys goods not in order to consume them but in order to sell them again for a profit. Indeed, the merchant does not desire the goods for their own sake. 'There is no limit to the end which this kind of acquisition has in view because the end is wealth in the form of the possession of goods' (*Pol.* 1257b); put another way, the number of woven tapestries that a consumption-orientated household needs is finite, whereas if tapestries are intended for re-sale – that is, treated as commodities – there is no obvious limit to the number that could be accumulated. Commodities are no longer 'embedded' in society or directed towards social ends, and all excess is dangerous.

Merchants helped to provide the goods 'without which society would not work properly', but they were more likely to be condemned for their association with objects that seemed to threaten social order, and blamed for the scarcity and cost of necessary commodities. Where we tend to resign ourselves to the inscrutable workings of an abstract market, with only occasional grumbles about the greed of supermarkets and oil companies, classical writers saw all market problems in terms of the vices of the individuals who operated the system. Aristotle's reaction to the processes of commoditisation happening around him did not thereby hinder the development of distributive systems, but such attitudes did to some extent shape the response of society to the traders on which it increasingly depended.

CHAPTER 4

Institutions and infrastructure

The Carthaginians inform us that they trade with a race of men who live in an area of Libya lying beyond the Pillars of Heracles. When they arrive at this country, they unload their merchandise, arrange it in an orderly manner on the beach and then, returning to their ships, light a fire. When they see the smoke, the natives come down to the beach, place on the ground a quantity of gold in exchange for the goods and retire once more to a distance. The Carthaginians come ashore and consider the gold; if they think it represents a suitable return for their goods, they gather it up and depart; if, on the other hand, it seems to them to be too little, they go back aboard and wait, and the natives come and add more gold until the Carthaginians are satisfied. There is perfect honesty on both sides; the Carthaginians never touch the gold until it equals in value what they have for sale, and the natives never touch the merchandise until the gold has been taken away.

(Hdt. 4.196)

We must keep any form of misrepresentation entirely out of business transactions: the seller will not hire a bogus bidder to run prices up, and the buyer will not hire anyone to bid low against himself in order to keep them down; and each of them, when they come to naming a price, will state once and for all what they are prepared to give or take.

(Cic. *Off.* 3.61)

If prizes were to be offered to the market officials for settling disputes between merchants justly and promptly, so that sailings were not delayed, the effect would be that a far larger number of merchants would trade with us and would do so with much greater satisfaction. It would also be an excellent idea to reserve seats in the front row of the theatre for merchants and shipowners, and to offer them hospitality occasionally, when the high quality of their ships and the merchandise they carry entitles them to be considered benefactors of the state. If they could look forward to such honours they would look on us as friends and hasten to visit us so as to gain the honour as well as the profit. Any rise in the number of residents and visitors would of course lead to a corresponding expansion of our imports and exports, and of the money received from sales, rents and customs.

(Xen. *Ways and Means* 3.12)

Ecological conditions and patterns of consumption create a situation where some form of distribution is desirable; they are not in themselves sufficient to ensure that distribution will take place. The potential profits of exchange had to be weighed against the potential for loss. Every merchant would have to make a calculation of whether the likely returns on shipping a particular cargo to a given port would cover the costs of buying the goods at the going rate, of transport (or maintenance and provisions for the crew, if he owned his own ship), of the interest on any maritime loan and of customs duties, alongside an estimate of how hazardous the journey was at the time of year. In some cases, for certain cargoes or particular destinations, it would clearly not have been worth the effort; the archaeology of distribution makes this clear, as the further a place is from the sea or a navigable river, the lower the levels of imported pottery (taken to be indicative of the level of import of more perishable goods). In other cases, the degree of uncertainty about prices in the destination port may have made the enterprise unduly risky, unless there was reliable information about a local food shortage or some other event – a festival, for example – likely to increase demand. Archaeology cannot, unfortunately, show variations in the 'connectedness' of a particular location from year to year, rather than century to century, but it seems all too likely that some places enjoyed only intermittent service.

Fourth-century BCE Athens could not hope to support the whole of its population on local production, but suffered increasing difficulties in guaranteeing adequate grain supplies after the loss of its naval supremacy and the empire (Garnsey 1988: 134–64). This is the context of Xenophon's proposals, dating from the middle of the century, which are expressly intended to make the city more attractive to merchants and thus to influence their decisions about which port to visit. Athens would become a better place in which to do business; higher prices might be obtainable elsewhere, but Athens would be able to offer comfortable lodging-houses, convenient places of exchange, a choice between a wide range of attractive return cargoes or a currency that was accepted across the Aegean, and even free entertainment. This might indeed have made a difference to a merchant's calculations of profit and loss, and after all Athens represented a more or less dependable market for grain; the effort involved in trying to maximise profits by checking if higher prices could be obtained elsewhere would not have suited every trader. The opportunity for steady, relatively risk-free profit and the assurance of a warm welcome might even have encouraged more traders to set forth, rather than (as the pamphlet seems to imply) treating the grain trade as a zero-sum game in which Athens' advantage could only be at someone else's expense.

Xenophon's pamphlet exemplifies the fact that ancient states had import policies rather than commercial policies (Hasebroek 1933; Cartledge 1983), to which we should add that they also had a clear interest in enhancing their revenues. However, this does not automatically imply that state actions had only a neutral or negative effect on the development of private distribution, but simply that any positive effects were unintentional. The history of the grain supply under the Roman Empire emphasises this point. One example is the development of the port of Ostia; funded by the state and prompted entirely by concerns about the grain supply of Rome, but (leaving aside what seem to have been flaws in the original Claudian design, so that it had to be developed further under Trajan) a benefit to merchants of all kinds of goods who had previously had to anchor outside the sandbar at the mouth of the Tiber (Meiggs 1973; Rickman 1991). Elaborate harbour facilities were not always necessary for trade to take place, but a port which could offer merchants protection from storms was likely to be more regularly frequented and thus to have an advantage both in ensuring its food supplies and in increasing revenue from harbour fees and customs duties. Cities accordingly invested in harbour facilities, and often in market buildings; these, by concentrating exchange activity in one place, made it easier to regulate and tax, but perhaps also benefited traders by advertising their location to potential customers (cf. de Ruyt 1983; Frayn 1993: 1–11, 101–8).

The most striking example of the state's pursuing its own goals but incidentally creating an infrastructure for trade is of course that of the Roman roads; built in order to facilitate the movement of troops, military supplies and strategic information, but available for use by all (Laurence 1998, 1999). Roads eased the passage of both goods and information between different areas, reconfiguring the landscape around them; in some cases intensifying existing traffic, in others – because they did not necessarily follow existing routes – creating connections where none had previously existed (Horden and Purcell 2000: 126–30). The construction of canals to improve connections to or between navigable rivers, again for purely non-economic reasons, was potentially even more significant; Marius built a canal to improve access at the mouth of the Rhône, while Augustus linked Ravenna to the Po estuary (Plut. *Mar.* 15.4; Pliny, *NH* 3.119). The effectiveness of ancient states' campaigns against piracy has been doubted, but it was clearly important for them to claim success, to be seen to respond to the concerns of the subjects (not least the urban consumers whose food supplies might be under threat) and, perhaps, to create a sense of security that would encourage merchants to venture forth (de Souza 1999). The larger the state and the wider its territory, of course, the more likely it was that its actions would favour the development of trade in general, rather than simply giving incentives to merchants to frequent some ports at the expense of others.

THE COSTS OF EXCHANGE

It is noticeable that Xenophon emphasises the importance of being able to offer the swift resolution of legal disputes, so that non-resident merchants were not forced to hang around in Athens waiting for justice (becoming liable for the 'metic tax' after a month) but could head off on their next voyage. Some of the most important costs in exchange were, so to speak, potential ones: the costs of enforcing an agreement or exacting compensation if the other party in the transaction should prove to be untrustworthy.

Shipwreck and piracy were not the only risks involved in trade, or even the most significant. Legal sources and literary evidence such as Cicero's comments above give some impression of the enormous range of ways in which people might try to cheat one another in order to gain an advantage in exchange; Plato, indeed, wished to exclude all haggling, let alone salesmanship and the taking of oaths to guarantee the quality of goods, from his ideal state, on the basis that they undermined any hope of good order and honest dealing (*Laws* 916–17). The marketplace was a fertile source of disputes; from the merchant's point of view, if the risk of being cheated or robbed – or falsely accused of sharp practice – was too great, or the cost of trying to protect oneself against it was too high, then it was better not to embark on a transaction in the first place. The development of any form of exchange beyond the small-scale, highly personalised exchanges between members of the same community depended on establishing a workable alternative to trust as a basis for proceeding. The historical plausibility of Herodotus' account of trade between Africans and Carthaginians has been doubted (Curtin 1984: 12–13); it is best understood as an attempt to imagine how exchange could conceivably take place between two different peoples in the absence of the institutions that had been developed in fifth-century Greece to manage the problem.

Economic theory, as has already been noted, relies upon various simplifying assumptions in constructing models of the workings of exchange; one of the most important is that exchange is 'frictionless' (North 1981: 5). In practice, this assumption is clearly unrealistic; all exchange involves what are sometimes termed 'transaction costs': 'the costs of measuring the valuable attributes of what is being exchanged and the costs of protecting rights and policing and enforcing agreements' (North 1990: 27). Herodotus' anecdote, however fictional, illustrates this point. Both parties have to invest considerable time and effort in discovering what value the other side places upon the goods they themselves have to offer, to establish an arrangement that suits both parties. Even so, the Carthaginians can have no idea, without expending further effort, of the purity and hence the actual value of the gold; we can only assume that the quantities on offer were so large or the Carthaginian goods so cheap that quality was not an issue – which would reflect the common Greek perception that some barbarian lands were simply overflowing with precious metals, scarcely valued by the local inhabitants.

In fact any transaction can be seen as 'asymmetrical' in this way, in so far as the seller normally has better information about the quality of the goods than the buyer. The more effort that the buyer has to expend in determining whether the goods are acceptable, in quantity or quality, and the greater the possibility of error or deliberate deception, the less likely that exchange will take place; the buyer will demand a lower price to compensate for the risk, which may not be acceptable to the seller, or will pull out of the transaction altogether.

The seller's main concern is that the buyer may seize the goods without paying. Herodotus does not explain why one party does not simply take the opportunity to cheat; in economic terms, at least, the benefits of doing so (free goods) might well outweigh the costs (a repeat transaction becomes much less likely), since neither party would be in a position to pursue the other for retribution. The real point of the anecdote is the implicit contrast with contemporary Greek practices; trust and honesty could exist and be taken for granted in transactions between two different groups of non-Greeks, whereas in Herodotus' own society, money and law had for the most part taken their place as the moderators of exchange. Modern commentators would see this as a sign of growing economic sophistication, but it could equally be presented as evidence of the decline of traditional social bonds.

Money and law are examples of 'institutions', 'the humanly devised constraints that shape human interaction' (North 1990: 3; cf. Morris 2001), which reduce uncertainty in exchange and hence reduce transaction costs. Institutions may provide tools for measuring the quality and quantity of what is being exchanged, or rules for the conduct of exchange, or mechanisms for detecting when the rules have been broken and for enforcing punishment. They reduce the costs to individuals and remove some of the risks of exchange. For example, the existence of a highly efficient enforcement system (Trading Standards Officers, say) will reduce the need for an individual customer to measure the quality of a good herself, because the likelihood of being caught and the potential consequences will tend to deter the seller from sharp practice. A combination of inefficient enforcement and inadequate measurement of goods, on the other hand, opens up wide possibilities for cheating and rule-breaking on either side, so that exchange may come to be seen as too risky and expensive. Differences can exist within a single society – compare the various grounds on which one would consider buying a second-hand car from the 'small ads' to be a far riskier proposition than buying a loaf of bread from the supermarket – but even more between societies; according to adherents of this approach, the nature and effectiveness of institutions are the keys to understanding the divergent paths of historical development, and to explaining growth, stagnation and decline.

Institutions, formal or informal but above all those developed and supported by the state – which possesses the greatest ability to establish, regulate and enforce them – are seen to be vital for the development of complex, impersonal exchange. In ancient history the economic role of the state has often been judged negatively; the lack of any conception of 'the economy' as something that needed to be managed and hence the lack of any concerted attempt at promoting economic development meant that its activities were limited to collecting and spending taxes, usually in an unproductive manner. As we have seen, state consumption could in fact be an important source of demand for goods that had to be distributed, and could support the development of essential infrastructure that reduced some of the costs and risks of distribution. Similarly, the development of institutions has throughout history rarely been driven by any coherent economic policy but more usually by the state's pursuit of its own interests, above all its involvement in the resolution of disputes and its interest in collecting its dues.

MEASURING GOODS

Standardised weights and measures – usually plaques of lead, marked with an official guarantee – are known from the Bronze Age (Hornblower and Spawforth 1996: 942–3, 1620–1). One might imagine that their original purpose was to determine what proportion of the harvest was owed to the state in tax; however, that would not hinder their employment in exchange, to enable the two parties to agree on what was being sold (in weight or volume) and to ensure that the buyer did indeed receive the quantity of goods that had been agreed (the fact that some weights appear to have varied from the official norm is another story). The state's insistence on the use of official weights and measures for all transactions in the marketplaces it controlled both asserted its power to make such stipulations – this may be especially relevant in such cases as Athens' imposition of its own system throughout its empire (Meiggs and Lewis 1989: 111–17) – and made transactions easier to regulate:

Anyone who fails to use the weights prescribed for wood is not permitted to sell charcoal or logs or wood; he is not allowed to sell these on Delos even if he has imported them there or even if they are on board his ship as cargo; he may sell only those goods which he has registered in his own name. (*IDélos* 509)

The primary purpose of official measures on Delos seems to have been to make it easier to collect customs dues; the inscription goes on to require merchants to declare to the *pentekostologoi*, the officials who collected the 'one-fiftieth' sales tax, the price at which they would sell their goods. Magistrates such as the Athenian *metronomoi*, the weight inspectors, seem to have been primarily concerned with trying to ensure honest practice in the marketplace; the use of a single agreed weight system would also make it easier for citizen consumers to compare the prices of different merchants (cf. [Arist.] *Ath. Pol.* 51). Merchants, who were always buyers as well as sellers, would equally benefit from the ability to measure the quantities of goods accurately and to agree a price on a unit basis.

Coinage was in many respects similar to weights and measures: it was issued and guaranteed by the state primarily for its own purposes (possible motives include the need to pay mercenaries and state employees, or a convenient way of exacting fines from citizens), the act of issuing it was symbolic of state power (every state wished to have its own coinage, while Athens naturally imposed its own system on the whole of its empire) and yet it had wide economic ramifications (generally, Howgego 1995; von Reden 1995a: 171–94). Money – not necessarily in the form of coins – can serve a variety of purposes: as a measure of value, a store of wealth and a means of payment. Each of these functions could be important for the development of exchange: encouraging the farmer to convert his surplus from perishable agricultural goods into a more durable form of wealth, offering an agreed basis for determining the value of goods to be exchanged, providing a practical alternative to barter and thus enabling exchange to take place at a distance and between strangers. 'That is why all items for exchange must be comparable in some way. Currency came along to do exactly this, and in a way it becomes an intermediate object, since it measures everything, and so measures excess and deficiency – how many shoes are equal to a house' (Arist. *Eth. Nic.* 1133a).

The advantages of coinage as a particular form of money are several, mainly to do with its ease of use. It is easier to conduct transactions involving fractions of a currency unit than those involving fractions of, say, cattle, which might otherwise be a perfectly acceptable means of measuring value. It is generally easier to use coins whose value is pre-determined and guaranteed by the state than it is to conduct transactions by measuring the purity and quantity of unminted precious metals, and it is easier to establish an exchange relationship, however arbitrary, between precious coins (gold, silver, electrum) and those of base metals which are required for small-scale transactions. One important question about the development of Greek coinage has been how early it included sufficiently small fractions of coins to be useful for everyday exchange rather than just large-scale activities such as purchasing land or a house; the evidence now suggests that 'small change' (still, however, silver, so not yet usable for really small transactions) was available from at least the mid sixth century BCE (Kim 2001). This tends to suggest that the use of coinage was spreading throughout society by this date. Currency speeds up transactions, while an increase in the level of exchange activity might encourage the adoption of currency.

Anyone wishing to buy coins, whether gold or silver, can do so at the stone in the place where the assembly of the people is convened; if anyone sells or buys coins in any other place, the seller will be fined the total amount of the sale and the buyer will be fined a sum equal to the total value of the purchase; all purchases and sales are to be made in coinage issued by the state, the bronze and silver coins of Olbia; if anyone buys or sells using any other coinage, the seller will lose the object of the sale and the buyer will lose the price that was paid; those who break this law will have to pay a fine to the magistrates. (*IKalchedon* 16)

The extension of particular systems of measurement across a wider area can also be seen as a stimulus to exchange, although for the most part it was the result of political developments and conquest rather than a response to economic pressures. Changing coins always involved a direct cost, generally of about 5–6 per cent, paid to the official money-changer; changing between different systems of measurement might not involve financial cost but it did consume time. One of the many complaints about Athenian fishmongers was that they insisted on being paid in high-silver coinage and giving change in inferior coin (Ath. *Deip.* 6.225b). The adoption of Athenian or Roman coinage outside their places of origin or the establishment of a more or less universal system of measurement in the western Mediterranean under the Roman Empire thus benefited traders, in so far as they had to spend less time familiarising themselves with and adjusting to different systems. This was, however, a very gradual development; some classical Greek *poleis* insisted on the use of their own coinage in all market transactions, partly because of its symbolic importance and partly, we may suspect, because of the profits to be made from compulsory money-changing (cf. Bogaert 1968: 323–31).

Ancient coined money was by no means the perfect, all-purpose token money of economic theory. Its quality and precious-metal content could be variable (sometimes by accident, sometimes as a result of a deliberate policy of debasement by the minting power). This was not necessarily a problem for local exchange if there was general acceptance of the face value of the coins – something which the state was normally determined to enforce (Howgego 1995: 125–37):

All the gold coins on which Our face appears and which are venerated to the same degree must be valued and sold at the same price even if the size of the image varies . . . If anyone should do otherwise, he shall be decapitated or delivered to the flames or put to death in some other manner. (*Cod. Theod.* 9.22.1)

However, variable metal content might add to the costs in moving from one currency area to another, if the rate of exchange proved to be unfavourable. There was no paper money or equivalent of medieval letters of credit; in order to transfer wealth between regions, it was necessary either to come to an agreement with an overseas contact to advance the money or to move large quantities of coin or goods (Andreau 1999: 20–2; cf. Cic. *Fam.* 3.5.4).

It is possible to see this latter deficiency as a cause of the more limited development of ancient trade in comparison with early modern Europe; on the other hand, it could be argued that the ancients possessed the financial instruments that they actually required to support their activities, and that the impediment to development lay elsewhere (Harris 2000). It was perfectly possible in Roman law for a debt contracted in one place to be repaid somewhere else if this was agreed between the parties in advance; the merchants carried the wealth in goods, to be converted into cash at the appropriate moment (*Dig.* 45.1.122). Even in the early modern period, as in the 'triangular trade' between Africa (source of slaves), the West Indies (sugar) and Britain (assorted goods such as cloth, salt, alcohol and firearms), it was regular practice for merchants to carry return cargoes rather than money (Anstey 1975; Hobhouse 1985: 84–7). Ancient money fully served the purpose, essential for the development of regular, large-scale inter-regional trade, of providing a basis for agreeing the value of goods to be exchanged and for relieving the parties involved of responsibility for assessing the value of the means of payment.

ENFORCING AGREEMENTS

The first essential responsibility of the state is control of the marketplace: there must be some official charged with ensuring that honest dealing and good order are established. (Arist. *Pol.* 1321b)

[. . .] and the traders weigh the wool they sell and weigh it without deceit; if anyone does not comply with this, he shall pay 20 drachmae for each [. . .]; the market overseer shall exact the fine; transactions shall last until noon. If it rains, wool should not be brought and [. . .] they shall not sell wool of a year-old sheep; if they do, the market overseer shall fine them 2 drachmae per day. The trader or the retailer is not allowed to sell wool or the gratings from fleece from any other flock but their own; anyone who sells wool from another flock shall be deprived of the wool and shall be fined 20 drachmae and the prytaneis will put everything that was for sale up for auction. (*IErythrai* 15; Arnaoutoglou 1998: 40–1)

Legal institutions and the different methods of enforcing compliance provide the parties in a transaction with greater security; they deter attempts at fraud or theft, and offer a relatively cheap means of dealing with defaulters. The state's perspective on law is, broadly, that it can thus keep the peace, retain its monopoly on violence rather than permitting private retribution, and protect its own interests and those of its citizens.

Predictably, given both the state's priorities and the widespread willingness to believe the worst of those who made a living from pursuing profit, many of the Greek and Roman laws relating to exchange focus on the control of unacceptable practices by traders, especially retailers. The main role of market overseers such as the Athenian *agoranomoi* seems to have been consumer protection, 'to supervise the goods for sale to ensure that they are pure and unadulterated' ([Arist.] *Ath. Pol.* 51); Athens also had magistrates with specific responsibility for the grain supply, including checking that the prices of bread and flour were proportionate to the price of grain, and that the loaves were of the correct weight. It was clearly assumed that traders would seize any opportunity to sell sub-standard merchandise (compare Ath. *Deip.* 6.225, on the ruses of the fishmongers of Athens), give short weight (by selling wet wool, for example) or try to avoid weighing the goods at all, or misrepresent the quality of what they had to offer. Athenaeus implies the existence of an Athenian law against rinsing fish to make them look fresh, telling the story of how one retailer contrived a fight and pretended to be injured, so that an accomplice had an excuse to pour water over him – and his fish. The existence of a blanket prohibition on making false statements in the agora is clearly directed against sellers rather than buyers (Hyp. *Athenogenes* 14). The right to bring an action for offences like supplying grain to a market other than Athens or making excessive profits on the sale of bread was not limited to those directly injured; any concerned citizen might bring a prosecution and benefit from half of any fine levied if successful; in theory a strong deterrent against merchants going against the perceived interests of the *polis*, or at least an additional risk to be considered.

However, legal structures played a much more positive role in the development of exchange by establishing the terms under which it could take place and providing the means for policing any infringements; they determined the parameters of normal behaviour and expectation. Exchange can scarcely be conducted on a regular basis without the existence of some form of enforceable property rights. The ability to possess an object without any restriction on what one can do with it, including disposing of it, is central to the development of individual exchange, as opposed to exchange carried out on behalf of and in the interests of the community; it would be interesting to consider the relationship between the approximately contemporaneous developments of commoditisation and property law in the early Greek *polis* (Morris 1986; Tandy 1997). The Athenian law of sale, stating that an item remained the property of the vendor until the price was paid, offered a basic but necessary protection for sellers; sale on credit was not excluded in practice, but it was regarded as if the vendor had embarked on a separate transaction to extend a loan to the purchaser (Harrison 1968: 204–5; MacDowell 1978: 138–40). What matters most is that the rights and obligations of each party are clearly defined; the evidence suggests that the Athenians successfully integrated both informal and formal structures of exchange to regulate their dealings (Millett 1990: 171–5).

Roman law developed much more flexible and elaborate procedures; the original legal procedure for sale known as *stipulatio*, in which every element of the transaction had to be formally specified in the contract, was supplemented, by the second century BCE if not earlier, by consensual procedures like *emptio venditio* (de Zulueta 1945; Johnston 1999: 77–81). In the latter, the parties had to agree on the price and on the object to be exchanged, but other elements of the transaction were assumed to be covered by the precepts of existing law; in particular, the assumption of 'good faith', a concept that was interpreted flexibly and in accordance with accepted commercial standards. In other words, the buyer was entitled to expect that, for example, a sack of grain would be free from weevils, without having to specify this; the seller was held responsible for everything on which he might reasonably be expected to possess knowledge, compensating for the asymmetry of most transactions. Consensual contracts had their limitations; for example, they did not recognise the sale of 'generic' goods such as 'a sheep' rather than 'that specific sheep' – but it was possible to solve that problem through the addition of a *stipulatio*. Roman law came to be capable of supporting such complex transactions as the sale of a share in the wine to be made from grapes currently hanging on the vine. It is not hard to see such developments as a reflection of the increasing scale and complexity of distributive activity under the Roman Empire, bearing in mind that Roman law was often reactive rather than pre-emptive, devising new and revised rules in the light of cases brought before the magistrates.

Other legal developments supported more elaborate practices in other areas of activity. The most obvious and important area is that of contract law, establishing the obligations of each party to perform actions in the future, such as the way that a loan should be used and the conditions under which it should be repaid. In fourth-century Athens these became increasingly standardised for different kinds of transactions, saving those involved the trouble of having to decide on the rules on every occasion (MacDowell 1978: 231–4).

The law, men of Athens, declares that merchants and shipowners should bring actions before the Thesmothetae if they have been in any way defrauded in the agora either in connection with a voyage from Athens to any other port, or from some other port to Athens; and it declares that those found guilty should be imprisoned until such time as they shall have paid over the fine that was levied against them, so that no one may do wrong to any merchant without fear of the consequences. However, where someone is brought into court for a case where there is no written contract, the law gives them the right to have recourse to a special plea, so that no one may bring a baseless or malicious action, but that court cases should be limited to those among the merchants and shipowners who have really been wronged. ([Dem.] 33: *Against Apatourios*, 1–2)

It was also becoming more common in court cases to present a written contract supplemented by witness statements – and, by the end of the century, just the written contract – rather than witness statements alone as evidence of what was originally agreed (Thomas 1989: 41–2; 1992: 89, 149). 'We make written contracts on account of our distrust, so that he who adheres to their terms may be able to obtain compensation from him who breaks them' (Aeschin. 1.161); acceptance of the credibility of written evidence, and faith in it as a fixed and neutral record, offered contracting parties additional security. In many Greek cities written contracts were registered with officials after they were agreed, giving them the greatest claim to validity and thus deterring breaches on either side (Arist. *Pol.* 1321b; Thomas 1992: 141).

In Athens, as in Rome, the contract did not have to cover all eventualities; it took for granted existing laws and practices. In both cases, too, the law provides historians with evidence not only for procedures and the normal (or ideal) operation of business but also for the many things that might go wrong. Much of the extant material on Athenian law comes from law-court speeches where the transaction has clearly gone awry in some manner, whether grain-merchants are being accused of breaking the laws against hoarding and speculation (Lysias 22) or merchants are being accused of trying to escape repaying their loans ([Dem.] 34). The Roman legal sources do not reveal actual cases, but the jurists were fond of giving examples to consider the principles involved, which can reveal astonishingly complex but certainly realistic situations. An extract from a discussion of a contract for a maritime loan, in which the merchant Callimachus had been expected to pay off his debt after selling his cargo at Brentesium (modern Brindisi), but had then decided to take another cargo back to Syria, with Eros, a fellow slave of the one who had loaned him the money, on board, reads as follows:

If Callimachus, having loaded the goods onto the ship, then remained behind [in Brentesium], when he had already agreed in the contract that the money should be repaid at Brentesium and taken to Rome, and if the ship then sank, can he rely on the agreement of Eros, who was sent with him and who had been given no other permission or authority regarding the money that was owed, after the date of the agreement, than to receive it from Callimachus and take it to Rome? (*Dig.* 45.1.122)

This example also highlights one of the major developments in Roman law relating to trade, that of agency (Aubert 1994). It is clear that a great deal of business, including extending loans and commanding ships, was undertaken by slaves and other dependants, often with considerable freedom of action and responsibility; the vital question for anyone entering into a transaction with such a party was how far their master could be held responsible for their actions, since a slave technically possessed nothing that could be drawn upon for compensation. Masters sought to limit their liability to the *peculium*, the sum of money extended to the slave with which to do business; creditors sought greater reassurance. The law gradually developed guidelines to cover more and more complex situations; it was noted, for example, that there were strong grounds for being able to bring a case against a shipowner for the actions of his captain, 'for the standing of a business manager can be established before doing business with him, but with a sea captain there may not be sufficient information or enough time for full consideration' (*Dig.* 14.1.1). Of course the owner could not be held responsible for the captain's actions if they had no connection with the terms under which the latter had been granted authority, such as borrowing money to trade when he had been appointed only to manage the ship – but that raised questions of whether the captain could borrow money to cover repairs and maintenance, and whether the owner was liable if he borrowed money on that pretext but diverted it to his own pocket. The use of the *servus vicarius*, the slave of a slave, created a need for yet more legislation to define liabilities clearly in advance of any transaction. Each party sought his own advantage, and the eventual balance would depend on relative bargaining power; if the risks in the transaction were too unevenly distributed, however, the contract would not be undertaken unless the potential returns for the exposed party were commensurate (Johnston 1999: 105).

The law here provided the tools with which individuals could establish the terms of their business, aiming to reduce the level of uncertainty in a transaction. It also provided a basis for dealing with the consequences of some of the other sources of risk and uncertainty in trade, such as shipwreck; not only in the standard terms of maritime loans, which provided that the loan did not need to be repaid if the cargo was lost at sea, but also in the Rhodian law of jettison, providing that the sacrifice of a merchant whose goods were thrown overboard during a storm should be made good by contributions from everyone else on board whose property and/or lives had been thus saved. Again, the jurists' test cases tend to emphasise the complexity, or potential for complexity, of business, while also revealing the existence of ancient salvage operations:

If, in the course of a storm, a ship was lightened by jettisoning the goods of one merchant, but then sank later on in the voyage, and the goods of some of the other merchants were then recovered by hired divers, the merchant whose goods were jettisoned is entitled to receive a contribution from those whose goods were recovered. (*Dig.* 14.2.4.1)

There are two important issues in considering the role of legal institutions in reducing transaction costs in antiquity. The first is the extent of their jurisdiction, in all the periods before Roman law and Roman citizenship were extended across the entire classical world: how far was the law able to deal with disputes between citizens and non-citizens, and what, if any, protection was extended to citizens when in foreign ports. Athens explicitly provided legal remedies for anyone, citizen or not, involved in trade to or from its port, but this could be seen as a reflection of its peculiar dependence on trade in the fourth century; its empire had previously offered the means to ensure that merchants serving the city's interests were not molested. The situation in other cities is not so clear. Some of the extant treaties between states, known as *symbola*, make explicit reference not only to the mutual recognition of legal rights of one another's citizens but to the business dimension of this: 'if any Milesian has a contract in Olbia, he shall have recourse to the lawcourts' (Arnaoutoglou 1998: 131). The treaties between Carthage and Rome recorded by Polybius include measures to protect the interests of Carthaginian merchants in different ports (3.22.9, 3.24.11; Whittaker 1978). Under the Roman Republic the right to make contracts that were enforceable in Roman courts was confined to citizens (and those with Latin status) and to those who had been granted the *ius commercii*; that is not to say that no trade could take place with non-citizens, but it was always at the buyer's own risk, and that would certainly have discouraged large-scale transactions (Ulpian, *Tit.* 19.4; Frayn 1993: 117–19). The gradual extension of citizenship, first through Italy and then through other parts of the Mediterranean, must have made a significant difference to the security of contracts and the cost of business.

The second issue is that of the speed and equity of enforcement, either of which might influence the effectiveness of the law in reducing transaction costs. Xenophon emphasised the need for swift justice to allow merchants to travel onwards rather than having to remain in Athens; compare the complaint in Lysias 17.5 about having to wait for a verdict. Changes were made to the Athenian system by the second half of the fourth century; historians have disagreed as to whether [Dem.] 33.23 implies that cases were now heard only between September and April (allowing merchants to spend the summer trading) or only between April and September (so that proceedings could be concluded within the sailing season), but in any event applications to bring a case were now being accepted every month, reducing the time that had to be spent waiting to lodge a complaint (Cohen 1973; MacDowell 1978: 231–4). At Rome justice seems to have been available all year round. As regards fairness, it is clear from law-court speeches that foreigners might feel themselves at a disadvantage in front of an Athenian citizen jury and would seek to emphasise both their own credentials and the need for questions of political identity to be set aside:

You are the same people who, when a man had been impeached before the assembly for obtaining large additional loans from the emporion and not delivering to his creditors their securities, punished him with death, although he was a citizen and the son of a man who had been general. For you hold that such people do an injury not only to those who do business with them, but also to your emporion; and you are right in holding this view. ([Dem.] 34.50–1)

In Rome, since contract cases would be considered only between people of the same legal status, the question is rather of the degree of bias in favour of members of the elite, both in the exercise of justice – something on which it is difficult to comment in the absence of court records – and in the development of the law (Johnston 1999: 112–32). Certainly the law on the sale of grapes on the vine seems to place by far the greatest burden of risk on the merchants rather than the grower, denying the former compensation unless the harvest is completely non-existent rather than just very poor (Morley 2000). The laws allowing a master to limit his liability for the actions of the slaves of his slave seem also to favour those who conducted business through such layers of dependants rather than those who had to deal with them.

There was also the question of cost. The increasing sophistication of the law and the complexity of its attempts to cover every possible eventuality created a need for expert knowledge, in drawing up a contract or attempting to bring a case against someone, which presumably could be met only by spending money on legal advice. The proliferation of legal authorities also meant that, before the codification of the law under Justinian, there might be genuine uncertainty or ignorance on the part of the judging magistrate about how to decide a case (Johnston 1999: 126–8). Legal institutions can be a source of, as well as a means of reducing, transaction costs. They may indeed provide an incentive for finding alternative solutions to disputes, such as the Athenian tradition of independent arbitration; the plaintiff could trade the possibility of complete victory for the avoidance of the possibility of total defeat, while also saving the cost of hiring someone to write his law-court speech.

CONTROLLING TRADE

Amytus stated that in the previous winter, as grain was expensive and these men [the grain wholesalers] before you were outbidding one other and fighting amongst themselves, he had advised them to cease their bidding war, judging that it would be beneficial to you, their customers, that they should purchase grain at the most reasonable price; for when they sold it, they were not permitted to add more than an obol to the price they had paid. Now, as witness to the fact that he did not tell them to buy up grain in order to hoard it, but only advised them not to compete against one another, I will bring before you Amytus himself. (Lysias 22.5–6)

The state acted to resolve disputes and to regulate payments and receipts; it also intervened more directly in trade and redistribution where it felt that its interests might be under threat, above all in the case of the grain trade. To put it another way, state institutions were not necessarily always in favour of trade and traders. Two different approaches to the task of guaranteeing the food supply are found in antiquity, in the two cities with the greatest supply problems, with very different consequences (Garnsey 1988). Post-imperial Athens sought to control the activities of grain traders by restricting their freedom of choice, insisting that anyone who borrowed money in Athens to buy grain had to bring their cargo back to Athens, and closely regulating the prices of flour and bread. These measures cannot have been too restrictive, even though the merchants' profits were potentially limited, since supplies continued to flow into the city; presumably Athens remained a reasonably profitable market, and was a reliable source of finance for trade even if the money came with restrictions on its use. Rome's problem was not the availability of grain but the lack of means for bringing it to the city; the emperors ended up following Xenophon's advice in aiming to attract merchants and shipowners into the supply system by offering tax concessions, citizenship rights and exemptions from civic duties in their home city. The laws relating to these privileges offer a striking conception of traders as, in a sense, public servants:

Traders who assist in supplying provisions to the city, as well as shipowners who service the grain supply of the city, will obtain exemption from compulsory public services, so long as they are engaged in activity of this sort; for it has very properly been decided that the risks which they incur should be suitably recompensed or rather encouraged, so that those who perform such public duties outside their own country with risk and labour should be exempt from annoyances and expenses at home; as it may even be said, that they are absent on business for the state when they serve the grain supply of the city. (*Dig.* 50.6.5.3)

Such incentives were clearly extremely attractive, as it proved necessary to develop further legislation to prevent people from trying to claim them without having a sufficient portion of their fortune invested in shipping (*Dig.* 50.6.6.8; Sirks 1991: 60–1). The state *annona* system (which also carried supplies to the army) is sometimes thought of as being in opposition to the development of private trade; in fact, the two were closely integrated, above all because the state depended on privately owned shipping to carry its goods. The state effectively subsidised the cost and assumed part of the risk of transporting goods to many regions; there is no evidence that contractors were paid below market rates, and they could make additional profits by transporting private goods alongside their official cargoes (and occasionally attempting to claim tax exemption on such goods as well as on state supplies) (*Dig.* 39.4.4.1; Mitchell 1976). State demands for transport encouraged the building of more and larger ships, which could also be used for private enterprise – although the larger grain ships were probably ill-suited to tramping along the coast with a mixed cargo (Casson 1995: 171–2; Houston 1988).

States might intervene in the workings of the economy for many other reasons. Exclusion from exchange could be used as a punishment, banning convicted murderers from the agora – both a civic and an economic space, of course – or banning the entire population of Megara from the markets of the Athenian empire (MacDowell 1978: 111; Thuc. 1.67). Attempts might be made for different reasons to control imports, exports or consumption habits; the sumptuary legislation of the Roman Republic, the emperors' bans on cookshops and restaurants (Toner 1995: 80–3), Hadrian's law to restrict the amount of olive oil leaving Athens (*IG* ii^2 1100, 1916), or this curious law from fifth-century BCE Thasos, conceivably aimed against speculation in 'grapes on the vine':

No one is permitted to buy the fruits of the vine on the spot, for mustum or wine, before the first day of the month Plynterion; anyone selling against this provision shall owe an amount equal, stater for stater, to the price paid, of which half shall be given to the *polis* and the other half to the prosecutor. Prosecution shall be brought according to the procedure for violence. When anyone buys wine in wine jars, the sale will be valid if the wine jars are sealed. (*IG* xii *suppl.* 347)

Finally, the state collected taxes and duties, and it is sometimes argued that these may have been a serious impediment to the development of trade; compare Cassiodorus' remark about sailors who feared customs-posts more than storms (*Variae* 4.19; Finley 1999: 175, 159). The alternative view is that the attention paid to such sources of revenue, and the profit to be derived from them – the right to collect the 2 per cent duty on imports and exports in Athens was sold in 401/400 for 36 talents, for example, though there were rumours that the auction was rigged (Isager and Hansen 1975: 51–2) – is a clear sign of the high level of trading activity in the classical world (Purcell 2005). Duties were levied on imports and exports, not on goods in transit, and would simply be reckoned into the merchant's calculation of price; they were more or less a known quantity. Further, although the state collected them in order to finance its own activities and not through any policy of redistribution for the common good, the state's pursuit of its own interests did in fact support the development of a significant part of the physical and legal infrastructure within which trade and distribution operated.

FINANCE AND ORGANISATION

Institutions are not created only by the state, although state institutions have the greatest coercive force behind them; the activities of merchants were also structured by institutions which they developed themselves on the basis of what the law could support. The most prominent and important example is that of finance. Recent studies suggest that a small boat and a cargo might be purchased for the price of a medium-sized farm; the situation depicted in Plautus' *Mercator*, where the father of the hero had sold his father's estate and gone into trade on the proceeds, may well have been typical (Rathbone 2003). Some cargoes, however, were well beyond the means of the typical trader; the cargo of spices described in the Muziris papyrus, worth about 7 million sesterces – seven senatorial fortunes – is an extreme example, but a large cargo of wine, textiles or grain must usually have had to be funded through loans, at high rates of interest. As one speaker in an Athenian law-court argued, 'The resources required by those who engage in trade come not from those who borrow, but from those who lend; and neither ship nor shipowner nor passenger can put to sea, if you take away the part contributed by those who lend' ([Dem.] 34.52).

The basic structure of maritime loans had been established by the fourth century BCE if not before (Millett 1991: 188–96; Andreau 1999: 54–6). They have two distinctive features. There is no limit on the rate of interest that can be charged, unlike other loans, and this is clearly because of the level of risk involved for the lender: if the cargo was lost due to shipwreck, or had to be jettisoned, the borrower was not obliged to repay the loan or to pay the interest. Up to a point, therefore, the loan operated as a form of insurance, allowing merchants to survive occasional disasters, but it is worth noting that only the cargo was covered; proper marine insurance was a much later development, apparently inspired by the fact that merchants were ceasing to travel with their cargoes (Millett 1983). Given the risks involved, making a living from maritime loans depended heavily on sound judgement and expert knowledge; those with the resources to finance such trade must frequently have relied on agents to manage their investments, as seems to have been the case with Demosthenes' father (Dem. 27.11). Quite as much as the merchant, the lender or his agent had to be able to calculate the risks of a voyage to a particular port at a given time of year; the profitability of the cargo was less of a concern, since the borrower would have to repay the loan with interest even at a loss to himself – except that a misconceived voyage increased the likelihood of default or fraud. Former merchants probably possessed an advantage in being able to make such judgements:

Men of the jury, I have now for a long time been involved in foreign trade and until quite recently risked my own life at sea; it is less than seven years since I gave up seafaring and, since I had a moderate amount of money, tried to make it work for me by making loans on overseas trade. As I have visited many places and spent time in your port, I know most of those who are seafarers, and I know these men from Byzantium very well, having spent much time there. ([Dem.] 33.4)

Athenian court speeches naturally emphasise the range of difficulties that might arise with maritime loans, but the institution continued more or less unchanged in its basic form into and throughout the Roman period. There were a few minor modifications. The practice of *stipulatio* could be used to refine the standard form of the contract, specifying where and how the money was to be repaid or adding additional safeguards for the lender. In one example money was lent provided that the venture was completed within the 'safe' sailing season, or the borrower would be liable to repay the whole loan and any expenses regardless of whether the ship was wrecked (*Dig.* 45.1.122.1; Sirks 2002). It is impossible to say how common such an arrangement may have been, but its clear purpose is to reduce the risks involved for lenders by combining different sorts of loans in a single contract. The biography of Cato the Censor recounts an alternative approach; Cato, acting through his freedman, became a partner in an association of fifty or so merchants, so that the money he invested was not hazarded on a single voyage (Plut. *Cato maior* 21.6).

Most of the extant evidence, including the Murecine tablets from Pompeii, shows that business was generally in the hands of slaves and freedmen and their slaves, acting as agents (though of course not every freedman was working on behalf of a patron) (Andreau 1999: 9–29, 71–9; Crawford 1980; Casson 1989; Garnsey 1981). There is little evidence for the existence of 'merchant financiers' both operating and financing trade (the Sulpicii of Puteoli, who appear on the Murecine tablets, may be the exception). The financier in the Muziris papyrus closely monitored the enterprise through his agents but still preferred to leave the business to an independent merchant (Rathbone 2003). The vast sums of money that financed trade remained largely in the hands of the land-owning elite: 'He who possesses the belongings of others can never really be a rich man. At that rate even the silk merchants, who receive their goods as a consignment from others, would be the wealthiest and richest of men' (Chrys. *Hom. II on Ephesians* 13.58).

Organisations of merchants seem to have been relatively uncommon. In both Greek and Roman law individuals might combine resources for particular ventures, but there is little sign of any ongoing investment in commercial enterprises (Rougé 1966: 423–35; Andreau 1999: 50–7). One of the limitations of the Roman law on association, *societas*, which determined the distribution of losses and profits between partners, was that it did no more than that; an agreement concluded with one partner did not in any way bind the other, unless it could somehow be demonstrated that the first was acting as the agent of the second (Johnston 1999: 106–7). However, it is not clear that this should be seen as a technical deficiency or limitation so much as a preference; the laws relating to the management of business through dependent agents was, as discussed above, developed in considerable detail by Roman jurists, and this seems to have been the preferred mode of business throughout classical antiquity. It is not obvious that the Romans, at least, lacked the commercial structures that they actually needed (Harris 2000).

Associations of merchants are known from the Roman period largely from inscriptions, above all from ports like Ostia and Puteoli; these refer to membership of associations like the *collegium* of the Shippers of the Adriatic or the *corpus splendidissimum importantium et negotiantium vinariorum*, the grandiloquent importers and wholesalers of wine at Ostia (Meiggs 1973: 311–36), and in some cases provide details on the rulebook and social activities of the association. The idea that such groups should be seen as forerunners of medieval guilds has been regularly dismissed, but one Egyptian papyrus does provide evidence for a group of merchants co-operating in business:

[They have decided] that all of them shall sell salt in the village of Tebtunis, and that Orseus alone has obtained by lot the sole right to sell gypsum in the aforesaid village of Tebtunis and in the adjacent villages, for which he shall pay, apart from the share of the public taxes which falls to him, an additional 66 drachmas in silver; and that the said Orseus has likewise obtained by lot Kerkesis, so that he alone can sell salt therein, for which he shall likewise pay an additional 8 drachmas in silver.

And that Harmiusis also called Belles, son of Harmiusis, has obtained by lot the sole right to sell salt and gypsum in the village of Tristomou . . . upon condition that they shall sell the good salt at the rate of $2\frac{1}{2}$ obols, the light salt at 2 obols, and the lighter salt at $1\frac{1}{2}$ obols, by our measure or that of the warehouse. And if anyone shall sell at a lower price than this, let him be fined 8 drachmas in silver for the common fund and the same for the public treasury . . . It is a condition that they shall drink regularly on the twenty-fifth of each month each one chous of beer. (*P.Mich.* v 245)

It is possible that the circumstances in Tebtunis were exceptional, with demand insufficient to support competition (the rules also seek to undermine the activities of outside merchants). Nevertheless, this group combined social and business activities, without clearly differentiating between them in their rule book, and it is possible that the social activities of other associations sometimes concealed similar arrangements. Even if they did not, the advantages that could be gained in terms of information and contacts through regular meetings with fellow traders for social and religious activities should not be underestimated.

THE EDUCATED TRADER?

The final topic to be considered is, in a sense, part of the infrastructure of trade: communication skills. Basic retail trade can proceed on the basis of, so to speak, the universal language of mime, but any more complicated transactions will require some form of common language and understanding. Potentially this involves another transaction cost: traders will either have to devote time to learning languages or will have to hire translators, not necessarily available in every port – or they will simply have been forced to restrict their activities to particular regions. The lack of reference to communication difficulties in ancient texts may suggest that this was not too great a difficulty; on the other hand, in the case of the Greeks this may simply reflect their cultural chauvinism and assumption that all speakers of foreign tongues were *barbaroi*. Herodotus' success in gathering information from Egyptian and Persian sources must reflect the availability of people with the ability to translate, either Greek merchants or native translators – whose services would also have been available to the merchants. However, the economic advantages of a *lingua franca* – the spread of Greek through the East and Latin through the West as widely used second languages, where they did not supplant native languages altogether (see Millar 1981) – are obvious.

Even if the need for linguistic knowledge declined over time, the importance of literacy increased steadily; the use of written contracts expanded rapidly from the fourth century BCE, to the extent that some legal procedures were impossible without a written contract, while the ability to keep tallies of merchandise and to send and receive letters was a definite advantage in monitoring prices and keeping a close eye on investments (Harris 1989: 17–18). Not every trader needed to be literate; one could hire a scribe or buy an educated slave (though in the latter case there would need to be some means of monitoring what was being written), or stick to small-scale local trade where writing was less of a necessity. Literacy, as well as resources, may have constituted the great divide between traders working the important routes and sometimes undertaking state contracts, and the smaller fry. Its importance in long-distance, impersonal trade does go against the image of literacy in antiquity being confined to 'the elite' (Bowman 1991). School exercises recorded in papyri from Egypt include not only snippets of literary texts and handwriting exercises, but this mathematical problem: 'the freight charge on 100 artabai is 5 artabai; what is the freight charge on the whole cargo of 1000 artabai?' (*P.Mich.* II 145). It is hard to imagine the children of the political elite being asked to tackle such a problem, and Plato offers confirmation of the existence of an educational divide: 'When we criticise or praise the upbringing of individuals and say that one person is educated and the other uneducated, we sometimes use the term "uneducated" of men who have in fact received a thorough education, but one that was directed towards buying and selling or the merchant-shipping business or the like' (*Laws* 643).

Writing, it has been argued, was much like money in the way that it could reduce transaction costs; money stored wealth, writing stored rights, obligations and knowledge (Hopkins 1991: 157). Just as trade played its part in spreading the use of coinage, so it may have promoted literacy; the Greek alphabet was developed from the Phoenician, doubtless on the basis of trade contracts, while Strabo describes the Gauls' beginning to write contracts on the Greek model as the result of their dealings with the colonists in Massalia (Marseilles) (4.1.5; Harris 1989: 45).

In conclusion, trade could proceed without literacy, or company organisation, or money or weights and measures, or legal contracts and procedures; the constant 'background noise' of short-hop mixed trading around the Mediterranean and into its hinterlands went on perfectly well without such institutions. However, the absence of them increased the risks of transporting large and/or valuable cargoes, of lending or borrowing money to finance voyages, of delegating authority to agents or travelling on someone else's boat, or it increased the time, effort and money involved in making an exchange. The development of widespread, regular connectivity, and of larger-scale trade, depended on the development of institutions and above all on the development of the state as consumer, underwriter of supplies and infrastructure, and establisher and guardian of law.

CHAPTER 5

Markets, merchants and morality

In modern discussions of trade, the term 'market' is more likely to be used to refer to an abstract, impersonal entity, in and through which 'market forces' dominate people's lives, than to indicate a concrete place where people buy and sell goods. The idea of a 'farmers' market' may seem tautologous to many inhabitants of continental Europe, let alone to the rest of the world, but in modern Britain and the United States the phrase has become indispensable as many of the original connotations of 'market' have been overlaid and as direct encounters between producers and consumers have become rarer. The semantic shift says something about the development of modern retailing and attitudes towards it; a visit to a 'real' market is now associated with a conscious rejection of the ethos of the 'supermarket' or with the exotic experience of holidaying in countries where people still buy fresh seasonal food every morning, rather than simply being part of our daily routine.

The ancient world had no conception of 'the market' in the abstract sense. Markets were familiar enough, from the fifth century if not before; indeed, there was a range of different sorts of markets, catering for different kinds of producers, consumers and goods. The tendency of prices in the market to vary was well understood, but it was not attributed to impersonal 'market forces'; on the contrary, it was seen as the direct result either of changes in supply (most commonly, due to harvest failure or glut) or of the greed of individuals. The various regulations and officials introduced by states to monitor and control the markets that took place under their jurisdiction were expressly designed to make individual traders responsible for what were, in the eyes of the state and probably of many of the citizens, the consequences of their decisions; the right to make a profit was not inalienable, if this would threaten the interests of the community. The fact that the individual merchant might be wholly blameless, simply trying to recoup his costs, was not accepted as an excuse for the anti-social effects of his actions. Such an attitude may reflect the greater simplicity of ancient markets and the limited number of links in the supply chain, such that it was apparently possible to identify individuals who might reasonably – in the eyes of the citizens, at least – be forced to accept responsibility for adverse tendencies in the market (see Lysias 22). It is certainly a clear example of the fact that the ancients did not share the modern acquiescence in the notion that 'the market' is impersonal, perfectly just and efficient, and not to be challenged.

MARKETS AND MARKETING

Classical antiquity offered a range of places and occasions for buying and selling. Every city had its *agora* or *forum*, the spaces in which citizens gathered for different activities associated with civic life; stalls could be set up there when the space was not being used for other purposes, and every city had rows of shops in the streets around. The larger the city, the more elaborate its facilities; Athens had both the agora in the city and the market in the Piraeus, the 'world apart' where foreign traders and goods were to be found, ideally (though scarcely in practice) kept at a distance to avoid the possibility of corruption by foreign influences (von Reden 1995b). Many Roman cities acquired purpose-built market halls, *macella*, for the retail trade of different foodstuffs (de Ruyt 1983). The city of Rome was large enough to have a whole range of specialised markets as well: the Forum Boarium for cattle and the Forum Holitorium for vegetables, both down towards the Tiber, the Forum Vinarium for wine (location unknown, but recorded in inscriptions of wine traders who worked there), the Forum Suarium for pigs, the Forum Piscarium for fish and the Forum Cupedinis, once a market for delicacies and later a more general provisions market (Robinson 1992: 131–2). Many of these may have been predominantly wholesale markets, though it was also possible to buy goods directly from the *horrea*, the warehouses down in the plebeian Aventine district. The emperors constructed monumental market buildings, such as the Macellum Liviae begun by Augustus, the Macellum Magnum built by Nero and Trajan's Market at the edge of the imperial Fora, which may have taken over the roles of many of the old markets as the spaces in which they were held became increasingly monumentalised. Different districts of the city probably had their own local markets, and of course there were shops and stalls everywhere.

By no means all markets were permanent, either in form or in availability. Peasants were closely associated with periodic markets – *nundinae* in Latin, since they were held on every ninth day (that is, once every Roman week) – which gave them the opportunity to sell produce, buy what they required and take advantage of the facilities of the city without spending too much time away from their farms (cf. Hodges 1988; de Ligt 1993a: 106–54). In some districts, at least, these periodic markets became linked into circuits, held on different days of the week so that merchants could move between them, maximising the number of potential customers – and probably also making it easier to gather together the surplus production, where it would not have been economical for the merchant to go to each farm individually (Morley 1996: 166–74). The contribution of peasant surplus production to the feeding of the cities is suggested by the degree of effort that some city councils might put into preventing local landowners from holding their own markets on their estates; if the peasants were not coming into the local town, it was feared, their produce might be shipped off to another market or sold at a higher price (de Ligt 1993b; cf. Shaw 1981).

It is not clear how far the authorities believed in the market as a place where competition between sellers would keep prices low; the fact that Plato wished to ban haggling in his ideal state suggests that he at least completely lacked this conception, which is basic to modern understanding (*Laws* 916–17). The little direct evidence that we have suggests that haggling and bargaining were common practice, if not completely ubiquitous; the negotiations between Dikaiopolis and his potential customers in Aristophanes' *Acharnians*, the competition between the sellers of food for the sacred geese on Delos (Reger 1994: 10–11) and the casual reference in one of Theophrastus' character sketches: 'If he buys a slave at a good price, after much haggling with the seller, he says "I wonder how sound the merchandise can be if I got it so cheap"' (*Char.* 17.6). Athenaeus records an attempt at bargaining with an Athenian fishmonger: 'If you ask him "How much are you offering those two mullets for?", he replies, "Ten obols." "That's too expensive, will you take eight?" "Yes, if you will buy the one next to it as well." "Sir, accept my offer and stop being childish." "At that price? Get out of here."' (*Deip.* 6.224f).

We have no evidence either way for such bargaining at the level of wholesale trade, which took place in more private surroundings, but the overall level of prices and the volume of supply in the district must have influenced the prices that wholesalers could obtain. Much would always depend on the relative bargaining positions of those involved; the need of the retailer for goods in order to stay in business, the wish of the trader to sell his merchandise and move on, or his capacity to store produce until the price improved.

The elaboration of systems of retail distribution, as seen in the city of Rome, is a reflection of the size of the city and of the multiplicity of its inhabitants' demands; enough fish was being sold to have a separate fish market. Trade was on a sufficient scale to support a series of intermediaries; goods passed through several different hands, each taking their cut, and were transported across sea, up river and through the city streets, each stage of the journey having to be paid for, before being made available to consumers. This is an indication of the profits to be made; but it must have been reflected in excessive prices simply to cover the costs of transport. In a smaller market, direct contact was possible between the original shipper and the consumer, but this was at the expense of more limited competition between suppliers, so there was less opportunity to bring prices down through bargaining.

From the merchants' point of view, the critical influence on their profits was the cost of obtaining goods in the first place. Attending the same markets as the peasantry gave them the opportunity to put together many small surpluses into a cargo large enough to be worth shipping, with minimal effort; they would benefit from peasants competing with one another to sell their goods, since generally small farmers lacked the facilities to store crops for market. However, this was not the only way of acquiring goods; the Italian evidence suggests that the large landowners preferred to sell their goods at the farm gate, passing on the costs of transport to the merchant and, perhaps, gaining an advantage by restricting the merchants' access to information about prevailing prices (Morley 2000). This must reflect the degree of competition between merchants for these large surpluses, especially for goods like wine, as does their willingness to take on the risk of harvest failure by speculating on grapes on the vine. It also emphasised the gap in social status between landowner and trader, as the latter attended the former at his farm much as clients attended the morning ritual of greeting, the *salutatio*, in his town residence.

THE TROUBLE WITH TRADE

To accumulate money through trade is sometimes more profitable, except that it is so risky, and likewise through money-lending, if only it was honourable. Our ancestors held this to be the case and established it in the laws so that the thief should be fined double and the usurer fourfold. You may judge from this how far they regarded the usurer as a less desirable citizen than the thief. And when they praised a good man, they praised him in this manner: 'good cultivator and good farmer'. Anyone who was praised in this way was thought to have received the highest possible commendation. In my opinion the trader is an energetic man and someone who is dedicated to accumulating money, but, as I said above, he is also someone who lives dangerously and is always on the verge of disaster. Out of the farmers are born the bravest men and the strongest soldiers; their profession is the most highly regarded and most secure. (Cato, *De Agricultura* preface 1–4)

As to the crops which are to be sold, take care that each is removed from storage at the proper time. Those crops which do not store well should be taken out and sold as swiftly as possible, before they spoil; those which can be stored should be sold when the price is high. For often stored crops will not only pay interest on the storage but will even double the profit, if you sell them at the right moment. (Varro, *Rerum Rusticarum* 1.69.1–4)

It might seem reasonable to wonder in what ways Varro, or his character, is not being a trader, but it is clear that, for the Roman elite, the distinction was absolute. The marketing of surplus produce was an essential part of estate management in Greece and Rome alike, to obtain cash with which the wealthy could support their political activities, including the large sums of money they were expected to spend on financing triremes, constructing public works, and the like; this was not held to be in conflict with the ideal of self-sufficiency (Osborne 1991). The Roman agricultural writers are full of advice on how to manage one's estate in order to maximise the opportunity for profit, but they are remarkably coy about the subject of actually marketing their goods. Varro does include marketing as one of the headings under which his characters will discuss the subject of agriculture, but, just before they get to that point – just after the passage quoted above on storage – the dialogue is interrupted by the breathless arrival of a slave to announce that the priest they were waiting for has been murdered. It is hard to see this as anything other than a deliberate evasion of the subject.

The elite disdain for 'trade' was almost absolute. Cato's preface is fairly typical in its contrast between the morally upright and martially inclined farmer and the avaricious, unreliable, permanently threatened trader; the only hope the latter might have for respectability, according to Cicero, was if he gave up business and invested his fortune in land (*Off.* 1.151). Greek sources offer the same idealisation of agriculture (e.g. Xen. *Oec.* 5.17) and the same view on the merchant's lack of military qualities – 'merchants can pile up money, but that doesn't qualify them to be generals' (Xen. *Mem* 3.4; cf. Plato, *Laws* 831) – and his failure or inability to behave properly towards his friends and his city (Reed 2003: 54–61). Xenophon's Socrates – who of course rejected the idea of charging fees for his teaching because it would feel like he was selling himself (*Mem.* 1.2) – discusses people whom it is not desirable to have as friends:

'What about the good businessman who is determined to make a great deal of money and so always drives a hard bargain, and who enjoys getting money but is reluctant to hand it over?' 'In my view he is even less desirable than the last.' 'What about the man who is so dedicated to making money that he has no time for anything that won't be profitable?' 'He should be avoided, in my opinion; he will be no use to anyone who associates with him.' (*Mem.* 2.6)

The passion for making money, apparently as an end in itself, was one of the main grounds for suspicion against merchants; such men had no control over their appetites, they made profit from the needs of others, they threatened the social order and they could certainly never be trusted.

Wealth should not be seized; the wealth that comes to us from the gods is far better. If a man acquires great wealth through violence or force, or if he steals it through his words, as often happens when a man's mind is clouded by the desire for gain and dishonour tramples down honour, the gods soon deal with him. (Hes. *WD* 320–5)

We must consider anyone who buys from wholesale merchants in order to retail immediately to be vulgar; for they would gain no profit from this without having to resort to outright dishonesty; and there is no form of behaviour that is less noble than lying. (Cic. *Off.* 1.150)

The prevalence of such attitudes in the surviving literary sources has been taken as further evidence for the limited development of ancient trade; not only were traders clearly to be excluded from the upper echelons of society, and thus from any political influence, but the elite who commanded the vast majority of disposable resources were involved in trade only as customers. The alternative approach is to dismiss the view of Plato, Cicero, and the like as a smokescreen, emphasising the fact that senators did in fact own large ships – our main evidence for the existence of a law restricting them to vessels just large enough for shipping their own agricultural produce comes from sources bewailing the fact that the law is now being flouted (Livy 21.63.4; Cic. *II. Verr.* 5.44–6) – and did in fact deploy their resources, via intermediaries, in financing trading ventures. Neither approach to this question seems wholly adequate; the one over-values and the other simply dismisses the influence of ideas and values on ancient economic behaviour. We need to develop a view of economic ideology as an inexact and often self-serving image of reality that could nevertheless influence and constrain the actions of individuals as if it were real.

Most of our sources are entirely unconcerned about the behaviour of real traders; their interest is in the proper behaviour of men like themselves, citizens and members of the political elite. It is clear that, however one actually obtained an income, it was risky to leave oneself open to the accusation of being a trader. Pericles' supposed practice of ordering his slave household manager to sell all his produce in one go at the prevailing market price rather than increase its value through storage might have been explicitly designed to allow him to condemn his more acquisitive rivals for indulging in practices befitting a trader (Plut. *Per.* 16.4). Most elite activity was rather more ambiguous. Owning ships might be acceptable, if you could claim that it was for moving just your own produce; likewise putting forward finance for trading ventures, especially if this was done through an agent, establishing an appropriate distance from the activity. The key point, however, is that such activities might still conceivably be labelled as unacceptable by political opponents, while more extreme disavowals of inappropriate means of making a living could be attacked on different grounds – Pericles was disparaged for excessive parsimony.

Political invective could in fact seize on any aspect of an opponent's lifestyle or actions to make a point, but the power of wealth, the means by which it was obtained as much as the uses to which it was put, was a particularly contentious subject in both Athens and Rome. The ideology of 'good gain' served to constrain the actions of individuals, up to a point; it thus served, in part, to reinforce the authority of the elite as a whole. The expectation that true aristocrats should not be too concerned about profit, for example, helped to enhance their social status and claim to power in a society where wealth could be seen as a source of disruption; similarly, the ability of late Republican landowners to believe that their market-orientated, slave-run villas had a direct connection to the four-iugera farm of Cincinnatus bolstered their claim to be guardians of Roman tradition and values.

EXCHANGE AND SOCIETY

In brief, formal institutions and the forces of supply and demand are not the only significant influences on economic behaviour. The reason why most individuals behave basically honestly in exchange is not the fear of retribution if caught; it is simply the expected standard of behaviour, fully internalised by the majority. An oath might be a far better guarantee of honest dealing than the threat of legal action. Reputation may be more valuable than profit: 'For you all know, I think, that men take out loans with few witnesses present, but, when they pay them back, they are careful to have many witnesses, so that they may win a reputation for honesty in business dealings' ([Dem.] 34.30). Formal institutions make impersonal exchange between complete strangers possible, but it is striking how often those individuals then seek to personalise and socialise the act of exchange; the effort which modern retailers put into creating the simulacrum of a relationship with their customers suggests the extent to which we do in fact long for such a connection (Peter and Olson 2004).

One of the best examples of this from antiquity is the way that the younger Pliny dealt with the wine dealers who had lost out because of the poor harvest:

I gave everyone back an eighth of the sum he had paid me, so that 'no one should depart without a gift from me' (*Aen.* 5.305). Then I made a special provision for those who had invested particularly heavily, since they had done me a greater service and since they had lost much more . . . Since some of them had already paid a large amount of what they owed, while others had paid little or nothing, I thought it would be unfair to treat them all equally generously when they had not been equally conscientious in paying their debts. So, once again, I gave back to those who had paid in advance a further tenth of the money owed. This seemed an appropriate way of expressing my thanks to each of them according to his merits, and of encouraging all of them not only to buy from me in future but to pay their debts. (*Ep.* 8.2)

Legally, Pliny was under no obligation to offer any compensation, but he had to live up to (and help to create) a reputation for generosity and a disdain for undeserved profit. His actions had an instrumental dimension; rewarding those who had been reliable business partners in the past and thus introducing an element of dependence and obligation into the relationship, emphasising the gap in social status between himself and the merchants, and hoping to attract more traders and thus increase the competition for his produce through a reputation for fair dealing. It is impossible, however, to disentangle these different motives and insist that Pliny acted only through self-interest or only because he was bound by the code of elite behaviour.

Other transactions were similarly multi-layered, with the social, economic and cultural inextricably entwined. It is not clear how far the elite's attitude towards merchants may have extended through society – certainly the merchants themselves did not regard their profession as demeaning, but instead celebrated it on their tombstones – but one response to conditions of general mistrust, for trader and customer alike, could be to establish a personal relationship. Anthropological studies of markets suggests that in practice they rarely if ever operate according to the principles of pure competition; prices are not set simply on the basis of supply and demand, but according to the relationship between the individuals involved in each transaction. Strangers can be charged more; favoured customers receive a better deal and are expected to be loyal in return; haggling is a performance, a ritual, as much as it is a genuine attempt at finding a price acceptable to both parties (Millett 1990). The attributes of different character types portrayed by Theophrastus are, more often than not, established through their failure to adhere to the codes of behaviour that were supposed to apply to relationships within the agora:

When the agora is crowded he goes to the stands for walnuts, myrtle berries and fruits and stands there nibbling on them while he's talking with the vendor. (*Char.* 11.4)

When he goes to the market he reminds the butcher of any favour he has done him, then stands by the scale and throws in some meat, if possible, but otherwise a bone for the soup, and if he gets it, good, otherwise he laughs and grabs some tripe from the table as he is leaving. (9.4)

When someone has bought goods for him at a bargain price and presents his bill, he says that they are too expensive and rejects them. (10.4)

If he sells something, he charges so much that the buyer can't recover his price of purchase. (10.7)

The fault that is most regularly pilloried is a failure to maintain an appropriate distinction between different sorts of exchange. 'If he sells wine, he sells a watered-down wine to a friend' (30.5); 'he makes a secret purchase from a friend, who thinks he is buying something on a whim, and then, once he's got it, he resells it' (30.12) (Millett 1990: 184). This character treats his friends as if he were a trader trying to fleece his customers; others act as if their friends were merely traders. How one behaves in the act of exchange, whether of a gift or a commodity, becomes a mark of one's quality as a citizen; the agora becomes a place of social as well as economic exchange, and character is evaluated as often as goods (von Reden 1995a: 105–46).

This equation of citizenship and exchange comes to work both ways; that is, just as exchange relationships are interpreted in terms of the expectations of society and shaped by social values, so society can be seen in terms of exchange. This can be a positive thing; in the dispensation of justice, for example, the process of determining an appropriate punishment mirrors the negotiation that takes place in deciding on the right price. Tragedy, von Reden has argued, stages the processes of civic exchange (1995a: 149–68). Just as frequently, however, the application of the market principle to society is condemned; justice based on the like-for-like of commercial exchange is seen to be destructive of the community. Social relationships founded on the model of market transactions are corrupt and corrupting. Hesiod ironically applies the metaphor of exchange to the parent–child relationship: 'the men of iron will not repay their aged parents for their nurture' (*WD* 187–9). Commoditisation, meanwhile, threatens to undermine the whole structure of society, as the traditional means of distinguishing the aristocracy from the masses are now within reach of any vulgar upstart with money; that, at any rate, was the perspective of the old elite who found their position threatened and their values called into question (Kurke 1991, 1999). Even among such groups, however, the metaphors of trade and exchange were unavoidable; the Roman concept of *existimatio* as a means of discriminating between true aristocrats and the rest derives from *aes timare*, denoting, among other things, the establishing of a relationship of exchange between property and money (Habinek 1998: 45–6). Attempts at establishing a system of values separate from the imperatives of the market were unable to expunge the influence of market exchange on the concept of 'value'.

The development of this discourse in classical Greece reflects the rise of systems of distribution that were clearly separate from, and sometimes opposed to, the traditional gift-exchange practices of the elite. Traders did not constitute a newly powerful class in opposition to the aristocracy; the available evidence suggests that they were mainly poor and often not only foreign but non-resident (Reed 2003). It was not their values, wealth or power, but the implications of their practices for the traditional values of the community and for the whole idea of 'value', that aroused anxiety. Perhaps understandably, then, the expansion of trade in both scale and importance under the Roman period seems to have had little effect on aristocratic attitudes, except for Cicero's grudging acceptance that one could distinguish between retail traders and those of greater financial weight, and that the latter might even become less socially unacceptable if they became landowners (*Off.* 1.151). The existence of some more wealthy traders, with a few even gaining entry to the provincial elite, did nothing to resolve the ideological and practical problems that the workings of the market created for ancient states.

These anxieties are still visible in late antiquity. In its early, most radical phase, Christianity had had concerns about the incompatibility of wealth of any kind and the path to salvation. As it gradually reached an accommodation with the wealthy, a number of their attitudes towards specific forms of acquiring wealth seem to have been absorbed; Ambrose echoes classical writers almost perfectly in his warnings about the risks, the injustice and the exploitation of other people's misfortune inherent in trade (*Off.* 3.6). Another regards all property as unrighteous since the act of exchange is invariably driven by avarice and the wish to swindle the person with whom one is dealing:

For in some cases we have a small amount of property, and in other cases a large amount, which we acquired from the mammon of unrighteous behaviour. How do we obtain the houses in which we live, the vessels which we use and everything else that supports our daily lives, except from the things which, when we were still Gentiles, we acquired as the result of avarice, or inherited from our un-Christian parents, relations or friends, who had obtained them through unrighteous behaviour – not to mention that even now we acquire such things, although we now belong to the Faith. For is there anyone who sells things and does not wish to make a profit from the buyer? Or who buys something and does not hope to obtain a bargain from the seller? Is there anyone who carries on a trade and does not do so simply so that he can obtain his livelihood through this? (Irenaeus, *Adv. Haer.* 4.30.1)

However, Christian writers do present a more nuanced range of views; John Chrysostom, as noted in chapter 2, was able to celebrate the uneven distribution of goods around the world as a divine encouragement to travel and communicate with other people, all made possible by the gift of the sea. And there was no aspect of life that could not be turned into an exhortation to goodly deeds and charity: 'O excellent trading! O divine merchandise! You can buy immortality for money; and, by giving up the things of the world that perish, you receive in exchange an eternal home in the heavens! Sail to this market, if you are wise, O rich man. If necessary, sail round the whole world to get there!' (Clement of Alexandria, *Quis div. Salv.* 32).

Trade did not cease because of Christian fears that wealth, unless given away, might bar the way to salvation, just as it carried on in the face of disapproval from philosophers and Roman intellectuals. The concerns of the literary sources say far more about the anxieties of their authors for the state of their communities and for their own position than they do about actual traders; but, at the same time, these concerns cannot be dismissed altogether. A complete history of trade in classical antiquity must try to take into account the role of the idea and image of exchange and the market, and its influence, however tenuous, on how people behaved in the agora or the forum.

CHAPTER 6

The limits of ancient globalisation

The development of systems of distribution in classical antiquity, in both scale and scope – the range of goods being distributed, as well as the distances involved – depended above all on changes in the level and nature of demand. That can involve a simple change in the aggregate demand for the same basic goods, and the evidence does suggest a reasonably steady increase in the population of the Mediterranean and north-western Europe from about the ninth or eighth centuries BCE until some time in the second century CE (Sallares 1991: 50–107; Frier 2000; Scheidel forthcoming). However, the vast majority of this population continued to support itself largely from its own production; distribution enters the picture only when it is required to support a population which has exceeded the carrying capacity of its locality, as an alternative to emigration or controls on fertility. Far more significant was the development of social complexity in archaic Greece; an aristocracy that sought to differentiate itself through distinctive patterns of consumption, and a state which deployed increasingly large resources in the construction of communal monuments and festivals and in warfare. Very similar patterns can be seen later in Italy, Spain and Gaul, as the locals gained access to new goods and new habits through contact with Greeks and Phoenicians (C. Smith 1998; Cunliffe 2001).

Archaeology can sometimes present too smooth a picture of these sorts of changes; it is clear from literary sources that the apparently steady expansion of distribution and the increase of material prosperity into the fourth century and beyond was in fact punctuated by periods of upheaval, such as the colonisation period and the crisis in Attica at the time of Solon. The developing systems of distribution and growing wealth may themselves sometimes have been sources of disruption; Hesiod's poem *Works and Days* presents a world in which traditional social structures are apparently being undermined by 'the lust for gain'. We do not have equivalent sources for the experiences of Italians, Spaniards or Gauls; the adoption of foreign goods as a means of marking out status may also indicate fierce social struggles within these societies, fuelled by contact with external systems of distribution. The replacement of a theory of top-down 'Romanisation' in the western provinces with one of the willing adoption of Roman habits by the local elites may well lead historians to underestimate the disruption this entailed for traditional social structures.

Distribution clearly expanded dramatically between the archaic period and the last centuries of the Roman Republic, in its geographical extent, its scale and the range of goods involved. It is much less easy to chart the changing balance between different forms of redistribution; that is to say, the relative importance of 'trade' as the form of distribution involving more or less independent professionals. Hesiod's world clearly includes the free exchange of commodities – he himself contemplates going into trade as a means of disposing of his surplus – but there is considerable dispute over the date at which 'commoditisation' took off in the Greek world, and about the extent to which other forms of distribution survived into the fourth century and beyond (Morris 1986; von Reden 1995a: 67–74, 105–26; Tandy 1997).

Much depended on whether the most powerful consumers preferred to guarantee their supplies by relying on directed trade and redistribution rather than calling on independent merchants; even at the height of the Roman Empire, many of the goods being shipped around the Mediterranean remained outside the market. On the other hand, as discussed previously, even the Roman *annona* depended on independent shipowners for its operations; the supply of the city of Rome and the army was inconceivable without a high level of existing private distributive activity. Further, many of the state's activities created conditions that were favourable for the development of trade. The clearest evidence for the expansion of the market in the Roman period, besides the dramatic increase in the numbers of shipwrecks, is the volume of coinage produced by the state; as Hopkins has argued, unless this increase in the money supply had been more or less matched by increases in the value of exchange activity, the only result could have been rampant inflation – something for which there is no evidence (1980). Further, at least in the case of the law, the actions of the state seem in part to be a response to the demands of traders and those who relied on them; more trade, and the greater importance of trade in guaranteeing the grain supply of cities, meant that states had to take account of such concerns.

TRADE AND DEVELOPMENT

Market exchange, and above all price, can be seen as a form of communication; merchants respond to the information they receive about the rates at which goods can be purchased and sold, and they adjust their behaviour accordingly. The same holds true for producers; the price they can get for their goods in the market tells them about opportunities for profit and should, according to the expectations of economic theory, determine their future decisions. That is to say, demand can also influence production through the medium of exchange. Modern claims for the power of trade as an agent of economic development rest above all on its influence on the way that farmers and other producers manage their activities, aiming to increase their marketable surplus and to orientate production more towards the demands of potential consumers.

The evidence, both from antiquity and from more recent times, suggests that peasant farmers are frequently unimpressed by the blandishments of the market, and that aiming for self-sufficiency may be an entirely rational strategy; agriculture is a sufficiently risky undertaking in any case, so that subjecting oneself to the vagaries of market prices twice over – in the price that can be obtained for the goods produced for the market, and the price at which the means of sustenance can then be acquired – entails an unacceptable level of vulnerability. Nevertheless, the development of new patterns of consumption and new levels of demand did present an opportunity to which at least some ancient peasants responded. The adoption of grains suitable for bread-making across the classical world meant that farmers could maximise the potential gains from marketing their surplus without seriously jeopardising their subsistence prospects – indeed, growing wheat alongside barley actually improved their position, as the fact that each crop preferred different growing conditions made it unlikely that both would fail in the same year. Some of the surplus thus marketed went to pay rents, debts and sometimes taxes – demands which may have forced some farmers into the market against their wishes (Hopkins 1980, 1995/6). Some of it, however, was spent on goods that could not be produced on the farm, including the occasional non-essential item of consumption like imported pottery, further fuelling the development of distribution (de Ligt 1990).

What clearly did not occur in antiquity was a significant move away from subsistence farming. The main response to market opportunities came from the much smaller group of more prosperous farmers and the great landed proprietors; the former had greater resources (and most probably could call on the labour of animals and/or slaves) to produce a larger surplus and to support a higher level of consumption, while the latter required large quantities of cash in order to support their position in society and disposed of resources far beyond the needs of subsistence. It is a striking reminder of the limits of market penetration in antiquity that even the thoroughly profit-orientated villa estates of Roman Italy and Egypt aimed to produce most of the goods required for subsistence and equipment themselves (Rathbone 1991; Morley 1996: 75–6). Nevertheless, it is on such estates that we find clear evidence not only of the production of a large surplus expressly for sale, including attempts to improve productivity and maximise returns, but of responsiveness to the demands of the market for particular goods. The characters in Varro's dialogues on agriculture show considerable awareness of the potential for profit in the particular habits of consumption – the dinners of the voluntary associations known as *collegia* are specifically mentioned – in the city of Rome. Elsewhere the evidence comes from papyri, as in the records of the Appianus estate in Egypt, and from archaeology: the arrival of wine from Gaul and Spain and oil from Spain and Africa in the deposits of Ostia from the first century CE onwards, and the spectacular, even industrial-scale, multiple units of oil presses in the countryside of North Africa, explicable only on the basis of heavy investment by landowners in processing oil – their own and probably their tenants' as well – which must have been inspired by the expectation of significant returns (Mattingly 1988).

The city of Rome was a large and lucrative market of about a million consumers, effectively subsidised by the state and drawing in supplies from across the Mediterranean. However, it is worth noting how limited the impact of its demands could be. There were many areas of central Italy, let alone more remote parts of the peninsula, that showed little sign of changing their agricultural practices in response to the profits to be made; the costs of transport and of obtaining market information restricted most of the influence of the metropolis to those areas with easy access to the sea. The inland areas of northern Etruria remained largely untouched by the changes that took place on the coast and in more southern regions, both the 'boom' of new (and often well-appointed) villa sites in the last two centuries BCE and the apparent decline of the later first century CE (Attolini *et al.* 1991). The impact of smaller cities, even those with a few hundred thousand inhabitants such as Alexandria or Constantinople, must have been even more localised.

In the modern world economy, it has been argued, the periphery (above all, the Third World) is kept 'underdeveloped' so that it can continue to serve as a source of raw materials and cheap labour and a market for the manufactured goods of the more advanced 'centre', rather than becoming a competitor (Wallerstein 1974, 1980; cf. Woolf 1990). In classical antiquity, the distinction between centre and periphery was clear in terms of their differential access to power and information, but there was no clear economic differentiation With the exception of a few areas with unique advantages, above all the immediate hinterland of big cities, centre and periphery pursued the same agricultural activities; the products of the latter were less likely to reach the market at the centre not because of a discriminatory system of tariffs and quotas, but because of the tyranny of distance in a pre-industrial economy. A few areas were privileged – though the impact of the city's demands might not be wholly positive – rather than any areas being especially disadvantaged.

GLOBALISATION AND ITS LIMITS

Even the more remote regions of the Apennines, the Balkans or the German frontier, let alone the distant north of Britain, have yielded significant quantities of imported Roman pottery, coins and other artefacts. Roman culture, or at least a standard repertoire of material goods and patterns of consumption, was spread across the empire, initially through the movement of armies and officials but increasingly through the voluntary adoption of 'Romanness' as an identity by natives. The culture of the empire was never homogeneous, and indeed it drew strength from its ability to absorb local traditions; there were as a result some significant differences in material culture between Britain and Gaul, let alone between the long-established cities of the East and the newly urbanised West. Nevertheless, similar patterns, in city design and architecture, in diet, in social structure, in dress, in social activities and in material goods, are found throughout the Roman world. Political unity brought with it a remarkable degree of convergence in the practices of everyday life, while the city of Rome was the place where the coexistent variety and unity of the empire were celebrated, reconciled and recycled (Edwards and Woolf 2003).

It is tempting to emphasise the analogy with our contemporary experiences by applying the label 'globalisation' to this process of cultural harmonisation. Long before the term had been coined, this had been Rostovtzeff's instinct:

The creation of a uniform world-wide civilization and of similar social and economic conditions is now going on before our eyes over the whole expanse of the civilized world . . . We ought to keep in mind that this condition under which we are living is not new, and that the ancient world also lived, for a series of centuries, a life which was uniform in culture and politics, in social and economic conditions. (1926: 10)

Whether the label is appropriate, or just another outburst of the modernising instinct, depends partly on our understanding of the nature of 'globalisation' as a modern process. One standard definition is that it refers 'both to the compression of the world and the intensification of conscious-ness of the world as a whole . . . both concrete global interdependence and consciousness of the global whole' (Robertson 1992: 8; cf. Waters 2001). Increasing cultural homogeneity is, according to this perspective, an effect of the process, albeit an important effect, rather than one of its constituent elements. It is easy to argue, however, that most inhabitants of the Roman Empire appear to have thought of themselves as members of the global com-munity that was the empire, and to have expressed this in their material practices as well as, in the case of the literary minority, in their writings.

The great difference between ancient and modern, however, lies in the driving forces of the two processes of globalisation – political unification on the one hand, economic interdependence on the other – and in the very different degrees to which the world was 'compressed'. The modern globe is effectively shrunk by the powers of virtually instantaneous communica-tion and fast, relatively cheap transport of goods and individuals (Harvey 1988). The Roman Empire was, in these terms, scarcely any smaller than the empires or patchworks of independent states that preceded it; communica-tion remained slow and expensive, with the abolition of political boundaries and investment in the imperial postal service offering only very marginal improvements. This clearly limited the possibility of economic integration. There are several obvious examples of ancient economic dependence, such as Rome's reliance on grain from Africa and Egypt; news of poor harvests would certainly affect the price of grain in the capital, once it eventually arrived, and would produce frenzied activity to find alternative sources of supply (Erdkamp 2005: 143–205). It is not at all obvious, however, that this constitutes economic *interdependence* to any significant degree, unless that is extremely loosely defined. Changes in the price of grain at Rome could not have the same effect on the prosperity of the regions that supplied it, unless the changes were large and prolonged, and even then they are likely to have affected the prosperity of certain individuals – merchants and large landowners – rather than the region as a whole. The capacity of other city markets under the empire, let alone those of earlier periods, to affect the fortunes of their suppliers was still less, proportionate to their smaller populations and reduced spending power.

Certainly there was no 'world grain market' in which changes in one part of the system resonated instantly throughout and affected everyone involved. At best, price changes in one specific market might affect another, but the effects were muted by the length of time it would take the news to travel, and the possibility of alternative sources of supply. If Egypt had suddenly been conquered by the Persians, one might suggest, the effects on the city of Rome would have been catastrophic, at least in the short term, but most of the empire could have continued as normal. The same can be said of the distribution of other goods; various cities and regions undoubtedly prospered because of their involvement in the supply of particular items, whether the textiles of Milan, the wine of Campania or the perfumes that were processed at Alexandria; however, very few – Ostia, certainly, and to some extent Palmyra – were wholly or even largely dependent on this trade for their survival. Producers in one area might respond to the tastes of consumers in another – this can be seen already in the archaic era, as Attic potters and pot-painters produced shapes and designs especially for the Etruscan market – but that is a very limited form of 'interdependence' (Osborne 1996). Regions might suffer from short-term shortfalls in supply, if the harvest failed or an army was suddenly billeted on them, and they might suffer from sudden shortfalls in demand if, for example, the army unit they had been supplying was moved to another frontier. The effects of such changes were localised and for the most part short-lived, since the market sector represented only a small portion of overall economic activity.

Classical antiquity was a world of networks and connections; people, goods and information moved freely and frequently, material conditions permitting (Horden and Purcell 2000: 123–72, 342–400; Morley 1997). The importance of this connectivity for the effective working of ancient society, and above all of some of the goods that were distributed, can scarcely be underestimated; the Greek or Roman worlds would have looked very different without wine, or imported fine-ware pottery, or incense. However, these were not ultimately essential for existence; the only items without which ancient society would truly have ceased to function effectively were land and the basic goods it produced, namely wood, iron and pottery, all of which were fairly evenly distributed across the world. There was no ancient equivalent of a commodity such as oil, supplied from a limited number of locations but entirely indispensable for the workings of the world economy, and the interdependence – and vulnerability – of the system was correspondingly limited. The only force other than the environment sufficiently powerful to produce lasting effects on the empire as a whole was the Roman state itself.

THE RETURN TO NORMALITY?

Who is so insensitive and a stranger to the sensation of humanity that they can be ignorant, or rather can have failed to notice, that in the business of selling carried on in the markets or in the daily activities of the cities, there is such unbounded license in prices that the uncontrolled lust for profit is not reduced either by abundant supplies or by successful harvests, so that men who are involved in this business without a doubt hope to predict the winds and weather from the movements of the stars, and are made miserable when the fertile fields are watered by rains from above, bringing the hope of a good harvest, since they consider that they have suffered a loss if there is an abundance of supplies because of good weather . . . (Edict of Diocletian on Maximum Prices)

'Our concern for humanity persuades Us to set a limit on the greed of such men'; thus declared the emperor in 301 CE (Frank 1940: 305–421; Williams 1985: 126–39, 128–32; Meissner 2000). The Edict is generally interpreted as a response to a short-term inflationary crisis which primarily affected those who received wages from the state in coin, namely soldiers and civil servants – hence the state's willingness to contemplate drastic intervention. This willingness was compounded, of course, by the conventional image of those who made a living from trade; merchants, it is said, are utterly unrestrained men who must be forced to recognise that the empire's problems are due to their lack of control over their own appetites. 'The money paid by the whole world to support the army in fact ends up bringing profit to despicable thieves.'

Diocletian's Edict is one of the most valuable pieces of evidence for prices in antiquity; not the absolute figures (which were clearly affected by inflationary pressures over the previous century) so much as the ratios between them. However, this is not the limit of its usefulness; it is also extremely revealing about the economic conceptions and assumptions of the ruler of Rome and his advisers. The authors of the Edict understood something of the usual workings of the market, expecting that prices should fall in times of plentiful supply; hence the decision to set a limit on prices rather than fixing them, 'for this would not be just, when many provinces do enjoy from time to time the benefits of the low prices that they long for'. They noted the importance of the universal promulgation of the law, so that those who travel from port to port know that there is no possibility of taking advantage of local variations. Most striking, however, is their lack of understanding of the phenomenon with which they were confronted – inflation – and their lack of any sympathy for merchants; the death penalty is prescribed not only for the seller who breaks the law and for the buyer who conspires with him to break the law, but also for the seller who withdraws his goods from the market as a result of the law, 'for the penalty should be as harsh for someone who creates poverty as for someone who takes advantage of it'.

The development of trade and distribution under the Roman Empire was spectacular, but ultimately limited. The dramatic expansion of activity in the last two centuries BCE slowed and then went into reverse: the total numbers of shipwrecks from the period 0–200 CE are only slightly higher than those from the late Republic, and thereafter they decline rapidly (Parker 1992; Meijer 2002). This evidence does tend to overstate the rate of contraction, through the under-representation of shipwrecks from Africa, when the evidence of amphorae and pottery shows that goods from this region were being widely distributed in the third century and into the fifth, and from the eastern Mediterranean (Carandini 1983; McCormick 2001: 83–114). Other material, including the traces of atmospheric pollution from metal production, points to continuing high levels of economic activity in the third and fourth centuries (Hong 1994; McCormick 2001: 42–52). Nevertheless, there is certainly no evidence of the sort of sustained year-on-year expansion of economic activity which is seen in the European economy from the early modern period (Saller 2002). The economy of the Principate experienced some measure of growth, but the great expansion of maritime activity had already taken place under the Republic. The archaeology of distribution reveals a similar pattern; between the second and the fifth centuries, both the quantity and the geographical distribution of pottery contract, especially in the western empire (Hodges and Whitehouse 1983: 20–53). The bulk of activity first shifted to the east, above all when the foundation of Constantinople diverted resources from Rome – it was possible to make two or three profitable journeys in a year from Egypt to the new capital, rather than the single voyage to Italy – and then it declined absolutely (on Constantinople, Cameron 1993: 12–32).

Consideration of the forces that had promoted the development of systems of distribution in the first place offers a way of identifying some of the possible causes of this development. Individual patterns of consumption may have changed; as McCormick notes, it is impossible to tell whether the absence of spices in Carolingian cuisine reflects a supply problem or a change in taste that was responsible for a decline in the trade (2001: 5–6). A more serious problem, however, was the fact that tastes had ceased to change – the 'Roman' way of life was prevalent in the western provinces by the third century – while local production had caught up with demand: goods which had of necessity been moved long distances in previous centuries could now be obtained more cheaply from nearby, and there were no markets for the goods that had previously been exported other than local consumers. The most striking example is the development of endogenous wine production in Gaul, so that the region ceased to import Italian amphorae and began to export its own products to Rome (which could happily absorb them in addition to Italian supplies). Similar patterns of local production replacing imports (and sometimes being exported in turn) can be seen in the pottery evidence from Gaul and Britain (where the disappearance of imported fine wares is taken as evidence of local self-sufficiency in grain production) (Woolf 1997: 193–202; Fulford 1984). The frontiers became increasingly (if never completely) self-sufficient by the third century, so one of the key drivers of inter-regional distribution declined in importance (Wickham 1988: 191–2; Whittaker 1994: 103–4). The Antonine plague of the second century reduced the population and thus aggregate demand for a whole range of goods; the increasing inequality of property, with a few wealthy men commanding vast resources, may equally have had an effect on the capacity of the masses to consume.

The structures of inter-regional exchange in the Roman Empire were not autonomous and self-supporting; they reflected the demands of those who commanded the greatest resources: the state and the elite. The emperors were concerned with supplying the army and the city of Rome, not with maintaining Italian agriculture or promoting trade. When it became clear that the incentives offered to shipowners to sign up to transport the *annona*, the state supplies, were failing to attract enough contractors to ensure a reliable supply – something which may itself reflect the declining profitability of inter-regional trade, as well as the greater attractions of the eastern route – the state turned to compulsion, making the service of the *annona* a hereditary obligation by the fourth century (Sirks 1991). The success of these measures is unknown, but the shift from offering incentives to participate to disincentives to opt out seems to reflect the same mistrust of merchants and others involved in trade expressed in the preamble to Diocletian's Edict.

If any person should acquire an inheritance that is under obligation to the compulsory public service due from shipmasters, even if he is of high rank the privileges of his honour will not assist him in the least in this regard, but he shall be obliged to perform this compulsory public service either in relation to the whole of his estate or proportionally. (*Cod. Theod.* 13.5.3)

Those whose ships were involved, willingly or not, in this public service were subject to increasing levels of scrutiny and suspicion:

Every shipmaster will know that he must either deliver the receipt for the delivery of the cargo he has accepted within two years, or prove the truth of the reasons put forward for his failure to deliver. (*Cod. Theod.* 13.5.21)

If there is ever an allegation about the force of the storms [which have, allegedly, prevented the delivery of the cargo], the shipowner shall produce for questioning under torture half of the total complement of sailors whom he is proved to have had on board his ship. (*Cod. Theod.* 13.9.2)

The distributions to the population in the capital had been expanded to include olive oil in the second century and wine and pork in the third; the motive remained the emperors' need for popular support, especially in the context of political instability and disputes over legitimacy, but this development must either have taken business from existing traders or been introduced to fill a gap. Increasingly, the state moved to what might be termed a 'command economy' (Williams 1985: 126). The regulations associated with the *annona* system again provide an example: 'materials for making suitable ships shall be demanded first from all the provincials; then the shipmasters will provide for the repairs each year from the exemption they receive on the tax owed on their pieces of land' (*Cod. Theod.* 13.5.14). The Later Roman state increasingly abandoned the use of payments in coin and reliance on the market to supply its needs in favour of requisition, especially at a local level, and grants of exemption from taxes and other duties. An independent shipowner could no longer count on making a living from state contracts; they were potentially profitable only for those who had most of their wealth invested in land and who would thus benefit from the exemption from other impositions.

Other, apparently purely political, decisions of the Later Roman state had significant economic effects. When a single capital city became a less effective means of maintaining imperial power, the emperors had little hesitation in redirecting their expenditure to other centres, closer to the frontiers, such as Arles, Milan and Trier – each of which became, for a time, a significant centre of demand, but far smaller than the concentrated demands of Rome and one that could be more easily satisfied from local sources. Rome remained the centre of activities for the landowners in the Senate, and thus a significant centre of consumption, but the overall level of expenditure there fell, taking the population and the level of demand with it (Durliat 1990: 110–23). Constantinople, as the new Christian capital, stimulated building activity and distribution in the east of the empire – but almost directly at the expense of the west (Sirks 1991).

There were also changes in the patterns of consumption of the land-owning elite. Holding local civic office increasingly became a burden in the later empire, and certainly became a less effective route to advancement than in previous centuries; the elite directed their attention instead to obtaining posts in the civil administration and to avoiding local duties (MacMullen 1988; Garnsey and Humfress 2001: 94–5). Investment in the built environment declined in the absence of competition for prestige and magistracies; wealth was increasingly focused on the church and on private estates, regardless of the consequences for the cities (Barnish 1989; Rich 1992). The elite continued to live lifestyles commensurate with their status, albeit with greater attention to private consumables like mosaics, art works and silver plate rather than public spectacle, but that was insufficient to support a large infrastructure of distribution. The primitivist image of trade in antiquity as confined largely to the small-scale transport of luxury items for the elite seems most appropriate for the level of activity in the later Roman Empire in the West.

The institutions of trade remained largely unchanged in the later empire. The expansion of the Roman citizenship to every free inhabitant of the empire in 212 CE meant that proper contracts could now be set up across the Mediterranean; the growing divide in legal procedure between two classes of citizen, the *honestiores* and the *humiliores*, on the other hand, may have reduced the attractiveness of conducting business with members of the elite (Garnsey and Humfress 2001: 88–95). The usefulness of coinage was potentially affected by progressive debasements by the state (Howgego 1995: 115–40). The evidence suggests that there was no direct connection between prices and the precious-metal content of coins – that is to say, prices normally, but not inevitably, rose after a debasement, but certainly not instantly. In any case, merchants could always raise their prices to compensate for the reduced value of the coins, but that involved at least an initial cost in ascertaining the precious-metal content. The greater threat, even if short-lived and generally ineffective, was the intervention of the state to try to force the market to conform to its expectations and desires.

The final question is whether connectivity itself may have proved too costly for the empire to sustain. Certainly the Later Roman state depended heavily on the movement of resources and above all on the availability of information for its normal operations, and this made it vulnerable if connectivity broke down, even temporarily (Schiavone 2000: 198). There is some evidence that the supply system of Rome, specifically the traffic up the Tiber from Ostia, was already reaching capacity in the first century; potentially, a food crisis might then occur because goods could not reach the city from the port, as well as in cases of harvest failure or poor sailing weather (Rickman 1991). The land-owning elite profited greatly from the state's investment in maintaining the integrity and connectivity of the empire, through their involvement in both production and the financing of distribution, so that by the late empire elite power was restricting the ability of the state to raise taxes sufficiently to maintain that integrity and connectivity (MacMullen 1988: 122–97). Finally, regular traffic between different parts of the empire undoubtedly played a part in spreading disease. The bubonic plague of the sixth century first appeared in the ports and was clearly spread by sailors and merchants; south of Damascus, it followed the lines of the Roman roads (McCormick 2001: 40–1). The scourges of plague and malaria both affected coastal regions above all, precisely the coasts that had given the Mediterranean world such a high level of connectivity. The shift of the centre of gravity of European civilisation to the north and west can be seen as a response to malaria and other diseases as plausibly as it can be presented as the result of the Arab invasions; it represents, in fact, a flight from the consequences of regular seaborne trade and communication.

The world of late antiquity began to turn inwards, towards self-sufficient rural estates and away from the market. It is important to note that this did not mean the end of all distribution. Even in the eighth century, pepper, cumin, and the like continued to reach Italy, and occasionally went further north; when Bede died in Northumbria in 735, he left pepper and incense in his will (McCormick 2001: 708–11). However, the volume of trade in these goods seems far smaller than in earlier centuries, and it seems to be predominantly in the hands of small, local traders; exotic goods were passed from trader to trader, rather than carried long distances by a single merchant, and one consequence would have been that a succession of mark-ups increased their price. What is missing from the early medieval period is the sort of trade associated with Athens or Rome, the regular, large-scale distribution of a wide range of goods, catering for a wide range of tastes and pockets. The 'decline' of late antique trade can also be seen as a return to the normality of small-scale, short-haul *cabotage* after the exceptional level of activity, and exceptional degree of dependence on traded goods, in classical antiquity.

Bibliographical essay

OLD DEBATES

Although historians are increasingly expressing the view that the primitivist–moderniser/substantivist–formalist debates have run their course and have ceased to generate new or interesting questions, the issues they address remain important and some of the major works remain well worth reading. Rostovtzeff's books on the Hellenistic and Roman worlds (1953, 1957) are still impressive, especially in their pioneering use of archaeological and visual evidence; it was the manifest material wealth of antiquity, above all, that fuelled the optimistic assessment of its economic sophistication. Finley's *The Ancient Economy* (3rd edn, 1999; first published in 1973) offers a bracing scepticism and insistence on the differences between ancient and modern; it and some of his collections of essays (1981a, 1985) still represent essential critiques of both modernising and latter-day antiquarianism, examples of which can be found in much more recent publications. Hopkins, operating largely within a modified version of the primitivist paradigm, offers stimulating examples of the use of abstract models and deductive reasoning to understand ancient economic processes (1980, 1983b, 1995/6). The papers in Garnsey, Hopkins and Whittaker (eds.) (1983), written at the point where archaeological evidence was starting to make an impact on the debate, are essential; the volume of archaeological material has continued to expand dramatically, but the issues involved in applying it to questions of historical economics have rarely been more clearly set out. The papers in Parkins and Smith (eds.) (1998) offer discussions of a range of topics and periods that go beyond the usual focus of the debate, and the first stirrings of discontent (especially in Davies 1998) with the conventional arguments.

NEW APPROACHES

The forthcoming *Cambridge Economic History of the Greco-Roman World*, edited by Morris, Saller and Scheidel, will in due course be essential; it offers broad chronological and thematic surveys, organising its material on the basis of Production, Distribution and Consumption rather than more conventional divisions such as Industry, Agriculture and Trade, and generally aims to set the agenda (including a certain bias on the editors' part towards New Institutional Economics) rather than simply reflect it. In the mean time, different attempts at starting new debates and employing new theoretical ideas can be found in more specialised articles in collections such as Lo Cascio (ed.) (2000), Lo Cascio and Rathbone (eds.) (2000), Mattingly and Salmon (eds.) (2001), Cartledge, Cohen and Foxhall (eds.) (2001), Aubert and Sirks (eds.) (2002) and Lo Cascio (ed.) (2003). Archibald *et al.* (eds.) (2001) is generally more conventional in its approach but directs attention to important evidence that is often neglected by historians focusing on Athens and Rome; Le Blois and Rich (eds.) (2002) offers a range of perspectives on the impact of the Roman Empire on economic structures. Scheidel and von Reden (eds.) (2002) draws together a mixture of older and newer articles that are generally hard to find (such as Hopkins 1995/6) and in some cases were printed here in advance of publication elsewhere. Another collection that promises to be highly stimulating, J. Manning and I. Morris (eds.), *The Ancient Economy: evidence and models* (Stanford, 2005), appeared just too late to be taken into account here.

SOURCES

There is a kaleidoscope of references to trade, exchange and the movement of goods in the ancient literary sources; Meijer and van Nijf (1992) offer a selection of the most important, all translated and with helpful notes. They struggle heroically against the bias of the evidence towards Athens and Rome, finding relevant material from across the Mediterranean – but at the expense of being able to offer only a sample of the wealth of Athenian and Roman material. There are many continuities in economic, social, political and cultural structures across classical antiquity, which frequently make it legitimate as well as convenient to draw freely from the whole range of ancient sources in considering a subject such as trade – provided, of course, that these sources are properly contextualised, and that the recognition of a certain degree of continuity is balanced with an awareness of the degree of variation across ancient societies.

Legal texts are a particularly important source of material for economic activity in its broadest sense. Arnaoutoglou (1998) includes many legal sources relevant to exchange and trade, drawing especially on epigraphy from across the Greek world and on Egyptian papyri; especially useful, at least for those who can translate Greek, are the detailed references to other examples of a similar kind. There is currently no equivalent work for the Roman period, but Johnston (1999) includes plenty of references to relevant sections of the *Digest* that can easily be followed up; once the sections related to trade have been identified (Books 14 and 45 are particularly useful), the problems that any would-be sourcebook compiler would face in trying to make a selection will be obvious.

Greene (1997) is still an excellent introduction to different kinds of archaeological evidence, including shipwrecks and amphorae; despite its focus on the Roman economy, many of the general comments are more widely relevant. Also on Rome, Giardina and Schiavone (eds.) (1981) offers a number of important chapters on the archaeology of distribution of different items, Peacock and Williams (1986) focuses specifically on the significance of transport and storage amphorae, and Tchernia (1986) offers a model for the combination of archaeological and historical evidence in studying the economic and social history of a particular commodity. Howgego (1995) is the best introductory guide to coinage evidence; Parker (1992) is the essential compendium of shipwrecks.

ECOLOGY

The two essential books on this theme are both thoroughly forbidding in size and complexity. Sallares (1991) includes essential discussion of the development of the relationship between humans and different kinds of grain, of demographic change, and of the impact of an ecological perspective on ancient history; it is, however, fairly technical, and does not consider trade specifically. Horden and Purcell (2000) is, as the footnotes to chapter 2 indicate, the work that is now pushing forward the debate; their most important contributions include the conception of the Mediterranean environment as 'unity in diversity' and the emphasis on the ubiquity of *cabotage*, while their extended chronological perspective, comparing the ancient and medieval worlds, is frequently fascinating and illuminating. The potential drawback is that their discussion of distribution is fully integrated into their overall argument, so that it is really essential to read the entire work rather than focus on certain sections, and they regularly postpone full discussion of particular issues to volume II, the date of whose appearance has yet to be set. Harris (ed.) (2005a) presents a range of responses to the work, many of which approach it from the perspective of trade and distribution.

CONSUMPTION

Several excellent books – such as Edwards (1993), Davidson (1997) – have studied the politics and social implications of consumption in Rome and Athens respectively. For full discussion of the economics of consumption it is necessary to wait for Sitta von Reden's paper in the new *Cambridge Economic History* volume due in 2007, though there is some relevant discussion in von Reden (1995a) and Foxhall (1998). Garnsey (1988) draws together the different themes as they relate to grain supply; Garnsey (1999) touches on a range of different aspects of the consumption of food.

INSTITUTIONS

The key works of the New Institutional Economics are North (1981) and (1990). These ideas are increasingly presented as the way forward for an economic history that can combine analytical rigour and the drive for generalisation with the traditional historians' respect for specificity and cultural difference; Morris (2001) offers an essential survey of the theoretical issues and an example of the way such ideas might be applied to ancient history. However, the view has also been expressed that NIE simply allows historians to carry on in exactly the way they had before, while using some economic-sounding language; the test will be whether more studies like that of Morris can demonstrate the capacity of this theory to generate new ideas and perspectives.

IDEOLOGIES

Most of the works on the ancient economy already mentioned touch on the economic ideas and concepts of antiquity, usually in terms of a sharp distinction between ancient and modern rationality. The little ancient material that can remotely be considered 'economic theory' is discussed in Meikle (1995). 'Cultural' approaches to understanding Greek economic behaviour are offered by von Reden (1995a) and Kurke (1991) and (1999); Habinek (1998): 45–59 presents a stimulating discussion of the role of the term *existimatio* in Roman discourse that emphasises the interaction of the economic and the political, which could be a model for future studies.

THE END OF ANCIENT TRADE

The debates around the 'Pirenne thesis', which argued that the precipitous decline of ancient trade can be attributed to the Arab invasions, are summarised in Hodges and Whitehouse (1983). Giardina (ed.) (1986) is still essential on the archaeological evidence for Late Roman trade; those who do not read Italian can find a review of the main arguments in Wickham (1988). Works such as Cameron (1993) and Garnsey and Humfress (2001) touch on economic issues, but the essential discussion of the economic aspects of the decline of the Roman system, lavishly illustrated with examples and anecdotes, is McCormick (2001).

References

Abulafia, D. (2005) 'Mediterraneans', in Harris 2005a: 64–93.

Adam, C. E. P. (2001) 'Who bore the burden? The organization of stone transport in Roman Egypt', in Mattingly and Salmon 2001: 171–92.

Andreau, J. (1999) *Banking and Business in the Roman World*. Cambridge.

Anstey, R. (1975) *The Atlantic Slave Trade and British Abolition 1760–1810*. London.

Appadurai, A. (ed.) (1986a) *The Social Life of Things: commodities in cultural perspective*. Cambridge.

   (1986b) 'Introduction: commodities and the politics of value', in Appadurai 1986a: 3–63.

Archibald, Z. H. *et al.* (eds.) (2001) *Hellenistic Economies*. London and New York.

Arnaoutoglou, I. (1998) *Ancient Greek Laws: a sourcebook*. London and New York.

Atkins, M. and Osborne, R. (eds.) (forthcoming) *Poverty in the Roman World*. Cambridge.

Attolini, I. *et al.* (1991) 'Political geography and productive geography between the valleys of the Albegna and the Flora in northern Etruria', in *Roman Landscapes: archaeological survey in the Mediterranean region*, G. Baker and J. Lloyd (eds.). London: 142–52.

Aubert, J.-J. (1994) *Business Managers in Ancient Rome: a social and economic study of institores, 200 BC – AD 250*. Leiden.

Aubert, J.-J. and Sirks, B. (eds.) (2002) *Speculum Iuris: Roman law as a reflection of social and economic life in antiquity*. Ann Arbor.

Bagnall, R. (2005) 'Egypt and the Mediterranean', in Harris 2005a: 339–47.

Barnish, S. (1989) 'The transformation of classical cities', *Journal of Roman Archaeology* 2: 385–400.

Berry, C. J. (1994) *The Idea of Luxury: a conceptual and historical investigation*. Cambridge.

Bocock, R. (1993) *Consumption*. London and New York.

Bogaert, R. (1968) *Banques et banquiers dans les cités grecques*. Leiden.

Bowman, A. K. (1991) 'Literacy in the Roman empire: mass and mode', in *Literacy in the Roman World: Journal of Roman Archaeology* supp. 3. Ann Arbor: 119–31.

Bowman, A. K., Garnsey, P. and Rathbone, D. (eds.) (2000) *The Cambridge Ancient History*, vol. XI: *The High Empire, AD 70–192*. 2nd edn, Cambridge.

Bradley, K. R. (1994) *Slavery and Society at Rome*. Cambridge.

Braudel, F. (1972) *The Mediterranean and the Mediterranean World in the Age of Philip II*, vol. 1. Translated from the 2nd edn, 1966. London.
(1981) *The Structures of Everyday Life: the limits of the possible*. London.
(1982) *The Wheels of Commerce*. London.
Breeze, D. J. (1984) 'Demand and supply on the northern frontier', in *Between and beyond the Walls: essays on the prehistory and history of northern Britain in honour of G. Jobey*, R. Micket and C. Burgess (eds). Edinburgh: 264–86.
Bresson, A. (2005) 'Ecology and beyond', in Harris 2005a: 94–114.
Bruni, S. (ed.) (2000) *Le navi antiche di Pisa: ad un anno dall'inizio delle ricerche*. Florence.
Cameron, A. (1993) *The Mediterranean World in Late Antiquity*. London and New York.
Carandini, A. (1983) 'Pottery and the African economy', in Garnsey, Hopkins and Whittaker 1983: 145–62.
Cartledge, P. (1979) *Sparta and Lakonia: a regional history 1300–163 BC*. London.
(1983) ' "Trade and Politics" revisited: Archaic Greece', in Garnsey, Hopkins and Whittaker 1983: 1–15.
(1998) 'The economy (economies) of ancient Greece', *Dialogos* 5: 4–24; reprinted in Scheidel and von Reden 2002: 11–32.
(2001) 'The political economy of Greek slavery', in Cartledge, Cohen and Foxhall 2001: 156–66.
Cartledge, P., Cohen, E. E. and Foxhall, L. (eds.) (2001) *Money, Labour and Land: approaches to the economies of ancient Greece*. London and New York.
Casson, L. (1989) *The Periplus Maris Erythraei: text with introduction, translation and commentary*. Princeton.
(1990) 'New light on maritime loans: P. Vindob. G 40822', *Zeitschrift für Papyrologie und Epigraphik* 84: 195–206.
(1995) *Ships and Seamanship in the Ancient World*. 2nd edn, Baltimore.
Castriota, D. (1992) *Myth, Ethos and Actuality: official art in fifth-century BC Athens*. Madison.
Chaudhury, S. and Morineau, M. (eds.) (1999) *Merchants, Companies and Trade: Europe and Asia in the early modern era*. Cambridge.
Cohen, E. E. (1973) *Ancient Athenian Maritime Courts*. Princeton.
Crawford, M. (1980) 'Economia imperiale e commercio estero', in *Tecnologia, economia e società nel mondo romano*. Como: 207–17.
Cunliffe, B. (2001) *Facing the Ocean: the Atlantic and its peoples 8000 BC – AD 1500*. Oxford.
Curtin, P. D. (1984) *Cross-Cultural Trade in World History*. Cambridge.
Curtis, R. I. (1991) *Garum and Salsamenta: production and commerce in materia medica*. Leiden.
D'Arms, J. H. (1981) *Commerce and Social Standing in Ancient Rome*. Cambridge, Mass.
Davidson, J. (1997) *Courtesans and Fishcakes: the consuming passions of classical Athens*. London.

Davies, J. K. (1998) 'Ancient economies: models and muddles', in Parkins and Smith 1998: 225–56.

Detienne, M. (1977) *The Gardens of Adonis: spices in Greek mythology*. Hassocks, Sussex.

Drummond, S. K. and Nelson, L. H. (1994) *The Western Frontiers of Imperial Rome*. London.

Duncan-Jones, R. P. (1982) *The Economy of the Roman Empire: quantitative studies*. 2nd edn, Cambridge.

(1990) *Structure and Scale in the Roman Economy*. Cambridge.

Durliat, J. (1990) *De la ville antique à la villa byzantine*. Rome.

Edwards, C. H. (1993) *The Politics of Immorality in Ancient Rome*. Cambridge.

Edwards, C. and Woolf, G. (eds.) (2003) *Rome the Cosmopolis*. Cambridge.

Erdkamp, P. (2005) *The Grain Market in the Roman Empire*. Cambridge.

Evans, J. K. (1980) '*Plebs rustica*: the peasantry of classical Italy', *American Journal of Ancient History* 5: 134–73.

Fine, B. and Leopold, E. (1993) *The World of Consumption*. London and New York.

Finley, M. I. (1981a) *Economy and Society in Ancient Greece*, R. Saller and B. D. Shaw (eds.). London.

(1981b) 'The ancient city from Fustel de Coulanges to Max Weber and beyond', in Finley 1981a: 3–23.

(1985) *Ancient History: evidence and models*. London.

(1999) *The Ancient Economy*. 3rd edn, Berkeley.

Fisher, N. R. E. (1989) 'Drink, hybris and the promotion of harmony in Sparta', in *Classical Sparta: techniques behind her success*, A. Powell (ed.). London: 26–50.

Forbes, R. J. (1955) *Studies in Ancient Technology*, vol. III. Leiden.

Foxhall, L. (1998) 'Cargoes of the heart's desire: the character of trade in the archaic Mediterranean world', in *Archaic Greece: new approaches and evidence*, N. Fisher and H. van Wees (eds.). London: 295–309.

Frank, T. (1940) *An Economic Survey of Ancient Rome*, vol. V: *Rome and Italy of the Empire*. Baltimore.

Frayn, J. M. (1979) *Subsistence Farming in Roman Italy*. London.

(1993) *Markets and Fairs in Roman Italy*. Oxford.

Frier, B. W. (2000) 'Demography', in Bowman, Garnsey and Rathbone 2000: 787–816.

Fulford, M. G. (1984) 'Demonstrating Britain's economic dependence in the first and second centuries', in *Military and Civilian in Roman Britain*, T. F. C. Blagg and A. C. King (eds.). Oxford: 129–42.

Garlan, Y. (1975) *War in the Ancient World*. London.

Garnsey, P. (1981) 'Independent freedmen and the economy of Roman Italy under the Principate', *Klio* 63: 359–71.

(1988) *Famine and Food Supply in the Graeco-Roman World*. Cambridge.

(1999) *Food and Society in Classical Antiquity*. Cambridge.

Garnsey, P., Hopkins, K. and Whittaker, C. R. (eds.) (1983) *Trade in the Ancient Economy*. London.

Garnsey, P. and Humfress, C. (2001) *The Evolution of the Late Antique World*. Cambridge.

Garnsey, P. and Saller, R. (1987) *The Roman Empire: economy, society, culture*. London.

Garnsey, P. and Whittaker, C. R. (eds.) (1983) *Trade and Famine in Classical Antiquity*. Cambridge.

Giardina, A. (ed.) (1986) *Società romana e impero tardoantico*, vol. iii: *Le merci. Gli insediamenti*. Rome and Bari.

Giardina, A. and Schiavone, A. (eds.) (1981) *Società romana e produzione schiavistica*, vol. ii: *Merci, mercati e scambi nel Mediterraneo*. Rome and Bari.

Gibbon, E. (1994) *The History of the Decline and Fall of the Roman Empire*, vol. i [1776], D. Womersley (ed.). Harmondsworth.

Gill, D. W. J. (1991) 'Pots and trade: space fillers or objets d'art?', *Journal of Hellenic Studies* iii: 29–47.

  (1994) 'Positivism, pots and long-distance trade', in *Classical Greece: ancient histories and modern archaeologies*, I. Morris (ed.). Cambridge: 99–107.

Greene, K. (1997) *The Archaeology of the Roman Economy*. 2nd edn, Berkeley and Los Angeles.

Grünewald, T. (2004) *Bandits in the Roman Empire: myth and reality*. London and New York.

Habinek, T. N. (1998) *The Politics of Latin Literature: writing, identity and empire in ancient Rome*. Princeton.

Harris, W. V. (1989) *Ancient Literacy*. Cambridge, Mass. and London.

  (2000) 'Trade', in Bowman, Garnsey and Rathbone 2000: 710–40.

Harris, W. V. (ed.) (2005a) *Rethinking the Mediterranean*. Oxford.

  (2005b) 'The Mediterranean and ancient history', in Harris 2005a: 1–42.

Harrison, A. R. W. (1968) *The Law of Athens*, vol. i: *The Family and Property*. Oxford.

Harvey, D. (1988) *The Condition of Postmodernity*. Oxford.

Hasebroek, J. (1933) *Trade and Politics in Ancient Greece* [German edn 1928]. London.

Healy, J. F. (1978) *Mining and Metallurgy in the Greek and Roman World*. London.

Herz, P. (1988) *Studien zur römischen Wirtschaftsgesetzgebung. Die Lebensmittelversorgung*. Stuttgart.

Hill, P. (1986) *Development Economics on Trial*. Cambridge.

Hobhouse, H. (1985) *Seeds of Change: six plants that transformed mankind*. London.

Hodges, R. (1988) *Primitive and Peasant Markets*. London.

Hodges, R. and Whitehouse, D. (1983) *Mohammed, Charlemagne and the Origins of Europe*. London.

Holton, R. J. (1986) *Cities, Capitalism and Civilization*. London.

Hong, S. *et al.* (1994) 'Greenland ice evidence of hemispheric lead pollution two millennia ago by Greek and Roman civilizations', *Science* 265: 1841–3.

Hopkins, K. (1980) 'Taxes and trade in the Roman empire', *Journal of Roman Studies* 70: 101–25.

  (1983a) 'Introduction', in Garnsey, Hopkins and Whittaker 1983: ix–xxv.

(1983b) 'Models, ships and staples', in Garnsey and Whittaker 1983: 84–109.

(1991) 'Conquest by book', in *Literacy in the Roman World: Journal of Roman Archaeology* supp. 3. Ann Arbor: 133–58.

(1995/6) 'Rome, taxes, rents and trade', *Kodai* VI/VII: 41–75. Reprinted in Scheidel and von Reden 2002: 190–230.

Horden, P. and Purcell, N. (2000) *The Corrupting Sea: a study of Mediterranean history.* Oxford.

Hornblower, S. and Spawforth, A. (eds.) (1996) *The Oxford Classical Dictionary.* 3rd edn, Oxford.

Houston, G. (1988) 'Ports in perspective', *American Journal of Archaeology* 92: 553–64.

Howgego, C. (1995) *Ancient History from Coins.* London and New York.

Isager, S. and Hansen, M. H. (1975) *Aspects of Athenian Society in the Fourth Century* BC: *a historical introduction to and commentary on the paragraphe-speeches and the speech Against Dionysodorus in the Corpus Demosthenicum [XXXII–XXXVIII and LVI].* Odense.

Jameson, M. H. (1977) 'Agriculture and slavery in classical Athens', *Classical Journal* 73: 122–45.

Johnston, A. W. and Jones, R. E. (1978) 'The SOS amphora', *Annual of the British School at Athens* 73: 103–42.

Johnston, D. (1999) *Roman Law in Context.* Cambridge.

Jones, A. H. M. (1974) *The Roman Economy: studies in ancient economic and administrative history,* P. A. Brunt (ed.). Oxford.

Jongman, W. (1988) 'Adding it up', in Whittaker 1988: 210–12.

Jongman, W. and Kleijwegt, M. (eds.) (2002) *After the Past.* Leiden.

Joshel, S. R. (1992) *Work, Identity and Legal Status at Rome: a study of the occupational inscriptions.* Norman and London.

Kim, H. S. (2001) 'Small change and the moneyed economy', in Cartledge, Cohen and Foxhall 2001: 44–51.

King, R., Proudfoot, L. and Smith, B. (eds.) (1997) *The Mediterranean: environment and society.* London.

Kleijwegt, M. (2002) 'Textile manufacturing for a religious market: Artemis and Diana as tycoons of industry', in Jongman and Kleijwegt 2002: 81–134.

Kopytoff, I. (1986) 'The cultural biography of things: commoditization as process', in Appadurai 1986a: 64–89.

Kurke, L. (1991) *The Traffic in Praise: Pindar and the poetics of the social economy.* Ithaca and London.

(1999) *Coins, Bodies, Games and Gold: the politics of meaning in archaic Greece.* Princeton.

Laurence, R. (1998) 'Land transport in Roman Italy: costs, practice and the economy', in Parkins and Smith 1998: 129–48.

(1999) *The Roads of Roman Italy: mobility and cultural change.* London and New York.

Le Blois, L. and Rich, J. (eds.) (2002) *The Transformation of Economic Life under the Roman Empire.* Amsterdam.

Lee, A. D. (1993) *Information and Frontiers: Roman foreign relations in late antiquity*. Cambridge.

Lewis, S. (1996) *News and Society in the Greek Polis*. London.

Ligt, L. de (1990) 'Demand, supply, distribution: the Roman peasantry between town and countryside', *Münstersche Beiträge zur antiken Handelsgeschichte* 9: 24–56.

(1993a) *Fairs and Markets in the Roman Empire*. Amsterdam.

(1993b) 'The nundinae of L. Bellicus Sollers', in *De Agricultura: in memoriam Pieter Willem de Neeve*, H. Sancisi-Weerdenburg *et al.* (eds.). Amsterdam: 238–62.

Loane, H. J. (1938) *Industry and Commerce of the City of Rome*. Baltimore.

Lo Cascio, E. (ed.) (2000) *Mercati permanenti e mercati periodici nel mondo romano*. Bari.

(ed.) (2003) *Credito e moneta nel mondo romano*. Bari.

Lo Cascio, E. and Rathbone, D. W. (eds.) (2000) *Production and Public Powers in Classical Antiquity*. Cambridge.

McCormick, M. (2001) *Origins of the European Economy: communications and commerce AD 300–900*. Cambridge.

MacDowell, D. M. (1978) *The Law in Classical Athens*. London.

MacMullen, R. (1988) *Corruption and the Decline of Rome*. New Haven and London.

Madeley, J. (2000) *Hungry for Trade*. London and New York.

Mann, M. (1986) *The Sources of Social Power*, vol. 1: *A History of Power from the Beginning to AD 1760*. Cambridge.

Mattingly, D. (1988) 'Oil for export? A comparison of Libyan, Spanish and Tunisian olive oil production in the Roman empire', *Journal of Roman Archaeology* 1: 33–56.

Mattingly, D. and Salmon, J. (eds.) (2001) *Economies beyond Agriculture in the Classical World*. London and New York.

Meiggs, R. (1973) *Roman Ostia*. 2nd edn, Oxford.

(1982) *Trees and Timber in the Ancient Mediterranean World*. Oxford.

Meiggs, R. and Lewis, D. (eds.) (1989) *A Selection of Greek Historical Inscriptions*. Reprint of 1969 edition with corrections and additions. Oxford.

Meijer, F. (2002) 'Wrecks in the Mediterranean as evidence of economic activity in the Roman empire', in Jongman and Kleijwegt 2002: 135–55.

Meijer, F. and van Nijf, O. (eds.) (1992) *Trade, Transport and Society in the Ancient World*. London and New York.

Meikle, S. (1995) *Aristotle's Economic Thought*. Oxford.

Meissner, B. (2000) 'Über Zweck und Anlass von Diokletians Preisedikt', *Historia* 49: 79–100.

Millar, F. (1981) *The Roman Empire and its Neighbours*. 2nd edn, London.

Miller, M. C. (1997) *Athens and Persia in the Fifth Century BC: a study in cultural receptivity*. Cambridge.

Millett, P. (1983) 'Maritime loans and the structure of credit in fourth-century Athens', in Garnsey, Hopkins and Whittaker 1983: 36–52.

(1990) 'Sale, credit and exchange in Athenian law and society', in *Nomos: essays in Athenian law, politics and society*, P. Cartledge, P. Millett and S. Todd (eds.). Cambridge: 167–94.

(1991) *Lending and Borrowing in Classical Athens*. Cambridge.

(2001) 'Productive to some purpose? The problem of ancient economic growth', in Mattingly and Salmon 2001: 17–48.

Mitchell, S. (1976) 'Requisitioned transport in the Roman Empire', *Journal of Roman Studies* 66: 106–31.

Morley, N. (1996) *Metropolis and Hinterland: the city of Rome and the Italian economy*. Cambridge.

(1997) 'Cities in context: urban systems in Roman Italy', in *Roman Urbanism: beyond the consumer city*, H. Parkins (ed.). London and New York: 42–58.

(1998) 'Political economy and classical antiquity', *Journal of the History of Ideas* 59: 95–114.

(2000) 'Markets, marketing and the Roman elite', in Lo Cascio 2000: 211–21.

(2001) 'The transformation of Italy', *Journal of Roman Studies* 91: 50–62.

(2004) *Theories, Models and Concepts in Ancient History*. London and New York.

Morris, I. (1986) 'Gift and commodity in archaic Greece', *Man* n.s. 21: 1–17.

(1987) *Burial and Ancient Society: the rise of the Greek city state*. Cambridge.

(1992) *Death-Ritual and Social Structure in Classical Antiquity*. Cambridge.

(1994) 'The Athenian economy twenty years after *The Ancient Economy*', *Classical Philology* 89: 351–66.

(2001) 'Hard surfaces', in Cartledge, Cohen and Foxhall 2001: 8–43.

Morris, I., Saller, R. and Scheidel, W. (eds.) (forthcoming) *The Cambridge Economic History of the Greco-Roman World*. Cambridge.

Moscati, S. (1968) *The World of the Phoenicians*. London.

Murray, O. (ed.) (1990) *Sympotica: a symposium on the symposium*. Oxford.

Nevett, L. (1999) *House and Society in the Ancient Greek World*. Cambridge.

Nicolet, C. (1991) *Space, Geography and Politics in the Early Roman Empire*. Ann Arbor.

North, D. C. (1981) *Structure and Change in Economic History*. New York.

(1990) *Institutions, Institutional Change and Economic Performance*. Cambridge.

Olshausen, E. and Sonnabend, H. (eds.) (1998) *Naturkatastrophen in der antiken Welt*. Stuttgart.

Osborne, R. (1991) 'Pride and prejudice, sense and subsistence: exchange and society in the Greek city', in Rich and Wallace-Hadrill 1991: 119–45.

(1996) 'Pots, trade and the archaic Greek economy', *Antiquity* 70: 31–44.

(forthcoming) 'Archaic Greece', in Morris, Saller and Scheidel (eds.).

Parker, A. J. (1992) *Ancient Shipwrecks of the Mediterranean and Roman Provinces*. Oxford.

Parkins, H. and Smith, C. (eds.) (1998) *Trade, Traders and the Ancient City*. London and New York.

Patterson, J. R. (1991) 'Settlement, city and elite in Samnium and Lycia', in Rich and Wallace-Hadrill 1991: 146–68.

Peacock, D. P. S. (1980) 'The Roman millstone stone: a petrological sketch', *World Archaeology* 12: 43–53.

Peacock, D. P. S. and Williams, D. F. (1986) *Amphorae and the Roman Economy: an introductory guide*. London.

Peter, J. P. and Olson, J. (2004) *Consumer Behavior and Marketing Strategy*. 7th edn, Boston.

Pitts, L. F. (1985) *Inchtuthil: the Roman legionary fortress excavations 1952–65*. Gloucester.

Polanyi, K. (1957) 'The economy as instituted process', in *Trade and Market in the Early Empires: economies in history and theory*, K. Polanyi, C. W. Arensberg and H. W. Pearson (eds.). Glencoe, Ill.: 250–6.

Pryor, J. H. (1988) *Geography, Technology and War: studies in the maritime history of the Mediterranean, 649–1571*. Cambridge.

Purcell, N. (1985) 'Wine and wealth in Roman Italy', *Journal of Roman Studies* 75: 1–19.

(2005) 'The view from the customs house', in Harris 2005a: 200–32.

Rathbone, D. (1991) *Economic Rationalism and Rural Society in Third-Century AD Egypt: the Heroninos archive and the Appianus estate*. Cambridge.

(2003) 'The financing of maritime commerce in the Roman Empire, I–II AD', in Lo Cascio 2003: 197–229.

(forthcoming) 'Roman Egypt', in Morris, Saller and Scheidel (eds).

Reden, S. von (1995a) *Exchange in Ancient Greece*. London.

(1995b) 'The Piraeus: a world apart', *Greece & Rome* 42: 24–37.

Reed, C. A. (2003) *Maritime Traders in the Ancient Greek World*. Cambridge.

Reger, G. (1994) *Regionalism and Change in the Economy of Independent Delos, 314–167 BC*. Berkeley.

Reinhold, M. (1970) *A History of Purple as a Status Symbol*. Brussels.

Rich, J. (ed.) (1992) *The City in Late Antiquity*. London and New York.

Rich, J. and Wallace-Hadrill, A. (eds.) (1991) *City and Country in the Ancient World*. London and New York.

Rickman, G. (1991) 'Problems of transport and development of ports', in *Nourrir la Plèbe*, A. Giovannini (ed.). Basel: 103–15.

Robertson, R. (1992) *Globalization*. London.

Robinson, O. F. (1992) *Ancient Rome: city planning and administration*. London and New York.

Rostovtzeff, M. I. (1926) *A History of the Ancient World*, vol. I. Oxford.

(1953) *The Social and Economic History of the Hellenistic World*. Reprint of 1941 edition with corrections. Oxford.

(1957) *The Social and Economic History of the Roman Empire*. 2nd edn, Oxford.

Rougé, J. (1966) *Recherches sur l'organisation du commerce maritime en Méditerranée sous l'empire romain*. Paris.

Rupprecht, H.-A. (ed.) (1993) *Sammelbuch griechischer Urkunden aus Ägypten*, vol. XVIII. Wiesbaden.

Ruyt, C. de (1983) *Macellum: marché alimentaire des Romains*. Louvain.

Sahlins, M. (1972) *Stone Age Economics*. London.

Ste. Croix, G. E. M. de (1981) *The Class Struggle in the Ancient Greek World.* London.

Sallares, R. (1991) *The Ecology of the Ancient Greek World.* London.

Saller, R. (2002) 'Framing the debate over growth in the ancient economy', in Scheidel and von Reden 2002: 251–69.

Scheidel, W. (1997) 'Quantifying the sources of slaves in the early Roman empire', *Journal of Roman Studies* 87: 156–69.

(forthcoming) 'Demography', in Morris, Saller and Scheidel (eds.).

Scheidel, W. and von Reden, S. (eds.) (2002) *The Ancient Economy.* Edinburgh.

Schiavone, A. (2000) *The End of the Past: ancient Rome and the modern West.* Cambridge, Mass. and London.

Schmitt-Pantel, P. (1990) 'Sacrificial meal and *symposium*: two modes of civic institutions in the archaic city?', in Murray 1990: 14–33.

Sekora, J. (1977) *Luxury: the concept in western thought.* Baltimore and London.

Shaw, B. D. (1981) 'Rural markets in North Africa and the political economy of the Roman Empire', *Antiquités africaines* 17: 37–83.

(1984) 'Bandits in the Roman empire', *Past & Present* 105: 3–52.

Sirks, B. (1991) *Food for Rome.* Amsterdam.

(2002) 'Sailing in the off season with reduced financial risk', in Aubert and Sirks 2002: 134–50.

Slater, W. J. (ed.) (1991) *Dining in a Classical Context.* Ann Arbor.

Smith, A. (1976) *An Inquiry into the Nature and Causes of the Wealth of Nations* [1776], R. H. Campbell and A. S. Skinner (eds.). Oxford.

Smith, C. (1998) 'Traders and artisans in archaic central Italy', in Parkins and Smith 1998: 31–51.

Snodgrass, A. M. (1980) *Archaic Greece: the age of experiment.* London.

(1983) 'Heavy freight in archaic Greece', in Garnsey, Hopkins and Whittaker 1983: 16–26.

Souza, P. de (1999) *Piracy in the Graeco-Roman World.* Cambridge.

Steingräber, S. (1980) 'Zum Phänomen der etruskisch-italischen Votifköpfe', *Mitteilungen des Deutschen Archäologischen Instituts, Römische Abteilung* 87: 215–53.

Stiglitz, J. (2002) *Globalization and its Discontents.* Harmondsworth.

Tandy, D. W. (1997) *Warriors into Traders: the power of the market in early Greece.* Berkeley.

Tchernia, A. (1982) 'La formule Pane e Vino Adjecto', *Epigraphica* 44: 57–63.

(1983) 'Italian wine in Gaul at the end of the Republic', in Garnsey, Hopkins and Whittaker 1983: 87–104.

(1986) *Le Vin de l'Italie romaine: essai d'histoire économique d'après les amphores.* Rome.

(1989) 'Encore sur les modèles économiques et les amphores', in *Amphores Romaines et Histoire Economique: dix ans de recherche.* Rome: 529–36.

Thomas, R. (1989) *Oral Tradition and Written Record in Classical Athens.* Cambridge.

(1992) *Literacy and Orality in Ancient Greece.* Cambridge.

Toner, J. P. (1995) *Leisure and Ancient Rome.* Cambridge.

Toynbee, J. M. C. (1973) *Animals in Roman Life and Art.* London.

Tracy, J. D. (ed.) (1990) *The Rise of Merchant Empires: long-distance trade in the early modern world.* Cambridge.

Veblen, T. (1970) *The Theory of the Leisure Class* [1899]. New edn, London.

Vernant, J.-P. (ed.) (1968) *Problèmes de la guerre en Grèce ancienne.* Paris.

Veyne, P. (1961) 'Vie de Trimalchion', *Annales: Economies, sociétés, civilisations* 16: 213–47.

(1990) *Bread and Circuses: historical sociology and political pluralism.* Harmondsworth.

Wallerstein, I. (1974) *The Modern World-System*, vol. I. New York.

(1980) *The Modern World-System*, vol. II. New York.

Ward-Perkins, J. B. (1971) 'Quarrying in antiquity: technology, tradition and social change', *Proceedings of the British Academy* 57: 137–58.

Waters, M. (2001) *Globalization.* 2nd edn, London and New York.

Weber, M. (1958) *The City.* [1920/21]. New York.

(1992) *The Protestant Ethic and the Spirit of Capitalism.* [1904–5]. London and New York.

Whittaker, C. R. (1978) 'Carthaginian imperialism in the fifth and fourth centuries', in *Imperialism in the Ancient World*, P. Garnsey and C. R. Whittaker (eds.). Cambridge: 59–90.

(1983) 'Trade and frontiers of the Roman empire', in Garnsey and Whittaker 1983: 110–25.

(1985) 'Trade and the aristocracy in the Roman empire', *Opus* 4: 49–76.

(ed.) (1988) *Pastoral Economies in Classical Antiquity.* Cambridge.

(1989) 'Amphorae and trade', in *Amphores Romaines et Histoire Economique: dix ans de recherche.* Rome: 537–9.

(1994) *Frontiers of the Roman Empire: a social and economic study.* Baltimore and London.

Wickham, C. (1988) 'Marx, Sherlock Holmes and late Roman commerce', *Journal of Roman Studies* 78: 183–93.

Wiedemann, T. (1992) *Emperors and Gladiators.* London and New York.

Williams, S. (1985) *Diocletian and the Roman Recovery.* London.

Winch, D. (1996) *Riches and Poverty: an intellectual history of political economy in Britain, 1750–1834.* Cambridge.

Wood, E. M. (1988) *Peasant-Citizen and Slave: the foundations of Athenian democracy.* London.

Woolf, G. (1990) 'World-systems analysis and the Roman empire', *Journal of Roman Archaeology* 3: 44–58.

(1997) *Becoming Roman: the origins of provincial civilization in Gaul.* Cambridge.

Wrigley, E. A. (1988) *Continuity, Chance and Change: the character of the industrial revolution in England.* Cambridge.

Young, G. K. (2001) *Rome's Eastern Trade: international commerce and imperial policy, 31 BC – AD 305.* London and New York.

Zulueta, F. de (1945) *The Roman Law of Sale.* Oxford.

Index